Flow Outside The Box

For Alia.

*For all young people everywhere who are just
beginning to step onto their Path.*

*And for anyone needing help navigating
their way back to The Flow.*

For you.

CONTENTS

INTRODUCTION ~ ix

1 | THE BOX ~ 1

2 | THE FLOW ~ 3

3 | THE MAP ~ 9

4 | SOURCE ~ 13

5 | EGO ~ 19

6 | PERFECTION ~ 21

7 | SUCCESS ~ 25

8 | FAILURE ~ 31

9 | CHALLENGE ~ 37

10 | PAIN ~ 41

11 | PERSEVERANCE ~ 45

12 | THE MIND ~ 51

13 | EMOTIONS ~ 63

14 | BODY ~ 71

15 | SOUL ~ 75

16 | INTUITION ~ 77

17 | QUIET ~ 81

18 | MEDITATION ~ 85

19 | THE PATH ~ 95

20 | HEART ~ 113

21 | COURAGE ~ 119

22 | TRUST ~ 121

23 | SERVE ~ 127

24 | BREATH ~ 131

25 | REVERENCE ~ 135

NOTES ~ 139

ABOUT THE AUTHOR ~ 157

ACKNOWLEDGMENTS ~ 159

INTRODUCTION

Joseph Campbell, the late, great mythologist, teacher and writer, spent his life studying comparative mythology and religion. He discovered a common thread woven through all, which he called "the monomyth." The archetype of human experience. A template of the human journey—the stages of the hero/heroine going on an adventure, facing a crisis, winning, and returning victorious. He realized, "If you really want to help this world, what you will have to teach is how to live in it. And that no one can do who has not themselves learned how to live in the joyful sorrow and sorrowful joy of the knowledge of life as it is."[1] My own journey has taught me just that—how to live in the beauty and the beast of this life, as it is. I've ultimately learned that our challenges are gifts which invite us to grow and thrive more joyfully in the present moment.

"Once you cross the great sea of suffering to reach the shores of liberation," states a spiritual principle, "it is your duty and obligation to get back in the boat and return to help bring others across." This book is a boat to climb into—a boat made of wisdom teachings from the many throughout history who have gone before across that great sea. Their wisdom, their boats, rescued me from drowning in the waves of life, and helped me return to The Flow. I now feel honored to stand in this long lineage and offer you a seat on the boat in the pages of this book.

"Don't believe anything," the Buddha is reported to have said, "simply because you have heard it, because it is spoken and rumored by many, it is found written in your religious books. Do not believe in anything merely on the authority of your teachers and elders. Do not believe in traditions because they have been handed down for many generations. But after observation and analysis, when you find that anything agrees with reason [personal truth] and is conducive to the good and benefit of one and all, then accept it and live up to it."[2]

If these teachings resonate with you, wonderful, use them. And when you "learn how to live in the joyful sorrow and sorrowful joy of the knowledge of life as it is," reaching the shores of liberation, please get back in the boat and go help others. If these teachings don't resonate with you, trust that. Life is not a one-size-fits-all. Trust your gut, your inner compass. It will not lead you astray. As the old adage goes, "There is more than one route to Rome." Continue to seek other routes, or boats, or ways, until you find the one which works for you. Inspiration, role models, and teachers are everywhere, all around you.

We are all here to help each other along this path of life. This life is a gift. Your life is a gift. "Yesterday is history. Tomorrow is a mystery. Today is a gift. That's why it's called, 'the present',," said a wise soul. From birth, others guide us, help us, mentor us, and coach us. At some point on your Path, you become the guide, help, mentor, or coach to others. Share your gifts. Pay it forward, in any way you can. Pass the torch. Light the way. We're all in this together.

_1_ | THE BOX

The proverbial Box is simply your comfort zone. It has six snug, secure sides. It's limited. It's confining. It's the predictable. It's the expected. It's what has _seemingly_ been tried before, tested, and proven—at least theoretically—to predictably work. Elders, such as parents, caregivers, teachers, family, community members, and bosses, unconsciously build The Box, often rotely, for younger generations to live in.

From birth, we are taught by these elders what is acceptable and not acceptable in The Box. For example, we are taught to value structure over creative flow. We are taught that book smarts are acceptable and rewarded but intuitive knowledge is looked down upon. We are taught to value doing over being. We are taught that expressing cheerfulness is acceptable, while expressing grief is not. We are taught that men can express anger, women cannot; women can cry, men cannot, etc. We are taught, for safety's sake, to stay in The Box, exhibiting only behavior which is acceptable. To do otherwise is risky, potentially dangerous.

For some, The Box feels like a good fit. For others, it feels confining, even suffocating. Carl Jung, the Swiss psychiatrist, and father of analytical psychology, observed, "The shoe that fits one person pinches another; there is no recipe for living that suits all cases. Each of us carries [their] own life-form—an indeterminable form which cannot be superseded by any other."[1]

Choosing to stay in The Box may feel safe, yet it might also pinch. And, more importantly, it can cost you the price of living a full and deeply fulfilling life. We must move to the edge of The Box and step out if we seek to grow, and blossom into our greatest potential. The writer Anaïs Nin, whose published diaries chronicled her private life, wrote, "Had I not created my whole world, I would certainly have died in other people's."[2]

2 | THE FLOW

The Flow is the tides and currents of the one, great energy field—Source. All that is. All that ever was. And all that ever will be. We are all swimming in it. We are all made of it. Everything is made of the same material of vibrating atoms in this great sea of Source. Everything—you, me, plants, rocks, animals, cars, stars, planets, galaxies. This one energy field is named differently from different perspectives: The One, The Great Spirit, The Divine, God, Yahweh, Allah, The Tao, Brahman, Universe, Universal Mind, and so on.

Because you are part of this energy field, at birth you are naturally pulsating in the currents of its Flow. Yet, as you become indoctrinated into this earthly realm, you are pulled out of this natural current by conditioning and others' demands to fit in with the expectations of what your generally well-intentioned caregivers and our collective society deem acceptable. The walls of The Box begin to grow up around you.

Because we need to fit in to survive, we seek and attach to external validation, and then habitually make choices based on external validation, which pulls us out of The Flow. Residing in The Flow requires that we let go of prioritizing what others think, and instead follow our own inner compass. We must also let go of any specific, conditioned ideas about how the outcome should look. We must let go of attachment to certainty, which is an illusion anyway. And we must release attachment to the belief that if we just do everything "right" by following "The Map" inside The Box, we can avoid pain and enjoy pleasure. When we let go, we are free. Free to flow.

When Rumi, the 13th-century Persian poet, penned, "Let yourself be silently drawn by the strange pull of what you truly love. It will not lead you astray,"[1] he was beautifully describing how to reside in The Flow.

Let me tell you the story of "The Little Beings." The Little Beings lived at the bottom of a very fast-moving river. It took all their might and energy to hold on against the current. Day after day and night after night they clung to their spot. One day, one of the Little Beings said, "I'm so tired of holding on. I can hold on no longer. I'm going to let go." And all the other Little Beings cried, "Oh no, don't let go! If you let go you'll be swept away forever. You'll die! Don't do it!" But he could hold on no longer. And he let go. As he did, the river's current caught him and carried him effortlessly to the top of the river. As he sailed along, he passed another group of Little Beings clinging to their spots at the bottom of the very fast-moving river. One looked up and said, "Hey, look, he's flying!"

The Flow is a natural state. The effort required to enter and stay in The Flow is to let go of clinging to The Box, and trust that this strange pull will not lead you astray. Simply let go and trust. This is not a new concept. It is an age-old principle, and one of the basic wisdom teachings which has been handed down through the ages. For example, Taoism, a philosophical and spiritual tradition originating in China some two thousand years ago, described "Tao" as the Source, pattern, and substance of everything that exists. Taoism emphasizes living in harmony with the Tao,

4

or the Way—The Flow—and becoming one with this rhythm of the Universe.

Imagine trying to walk up a down escalator. This is the feeling you have when you aren't in The Flow. You must exert a lot of focused effort. Now imagine walking on one of those moving sidewalks at the airport. This is what it feels like when you are in The Flow. You are exerting natural effort, but this effort is being met and it feels more effortless to gain ground. It's reciprocal and generative. Sure, you can eventually get up that down escalator, but it requires so much more effort. "The fates lead those who will, those who won't, they drag,"[2] mused the Roman philosopher Seneca, who was born nearly 2,000 years ago. "If you're falling, dive,"[3] interpreted Joseph Campbell. Go with The Flow.

Letting go creates freedom and ease. It is natural to want to cling onto things we want, but this grasping is exhausting and creates suffering. Imagine a garden hose. If you cling so tightly to it, you restrict the flow of water. Likewise, when you cling so tightly to life—people, things, circumstances, etc.— you restrict your ability to flow. If you are clinging to the "good" of a past moment, you inhibit and prevent space to receive the "good" of the present moment.

This moment will be replaced by the next, and then the next, and the next. Each moment contains all you need. Yet the form of all you need changes, morphs, and evolves as you change, morph, and evolve. "Everything that you love, you will eventually lose, but in the end, love will return in a different form,"[4] perceived Franz Kafka, the 19th century Czech-born writer. Life morphs and changes and evolves, moment by moment. Attachment to things, people, and outcomes pulls you out of The Flow.

Sir Richard Branson, the English entrepreneur, and founder of the Virgin Group with over 400 companies under its umbrella, and knighted by Queen Elizabeth II for "services to entrepreneurship," said, "In order to grow, you must be able to let go."[5] Wanna grow? Wanna evolve? Let go. A Zen Proverb states, "Knowledge is learning something every day. Wisdom is letting something go every day."

Letting go and surrendering to The Flow can feel frightening because we have been conditioned to stay inside The Box and follow "The Map" that guides us around inside The Box. Our minds have often been programmed to believe that The Map inside The Box is The Right Path. The One And Only Right Path which will lead to success and happiness. Follow The Map. Stay in The Box. Color inside the lines.

Yet, ultimately, "the right path" is unique to you, to each of us. It's unknown. Your own individual Path will be created with every step you take. It's created by each choice you make in the present moment. Your Path unfolds mysteriously before you, one step at a time. You cannot see the end of your Path because of all the unpredictable influences along the way. And thank heaven for that because if you knew your Path—if you could see the whole thing laid out in front of you to the end—what would be the fun of life? Life is a mysterious, unpredictable, and exhilarating ride. Trying to make it predictable is futile and life-dulling.

The Dutch post-Impressionist artist and painter Vincent Van Gogh, who posthumously became one of the most influential figures in the history of Western art, said, "I would rather die of passion than boredom."[6]

The Flow takes you to your "sweet spot," which is the intersection of what you like, what you are good at, and how you can help the world. Allow yourself to be pulled into that sweet spot of The Flow. This is where you feel your best, your bliss, most passionate, most alive.

Your inner guidance will lead you so that you will be drawn to deeply fulfilling experiences. Like a plant drawn to a sunbeam. It is a Path that only you can recognize by the way it makes you feel inside. It just feels right. As we live life, we become more attuned to what is right for us. Others may share what has worked for them, but only we can know what truly makes us feel inspired, awakened, connected, and alive. This sense of knowing is your inner compass.

Oprah Winfrey, the American television producer, author, actress, and interview host, was born into poverty in rural Mississippi to a single teenage mother, and landed a job in radio while still in high school. By 19, she was co-anchor for the local evening news. At 32, The Oprah Winfrey Show debuted, and ran in national syndication for 25 years as the highest-rated television program of its kind in history. By age 54 she had formed her own network, OWN, the Oprah Winfrey Network. She shared, "The first day I was on the air doing my first talk show back in 1978, it felt like breathing, which is what your true passion should feel like. It should be so natural to you."[7]

Allow yourself to be silently drawn by the strange pull of what you truly love, into your sweet spot and where you are naturally meant to be. Let go of The Map in The Box and allow yourself to flow from your inner compass. You do not have to stay inside The Box. There is a big, wide, sparkling world out there for you to explore, full of magic and awe.

3 | THE MAP

"The Map" inside The Box contains directions on how to stay in the safe confines of The Box. The beaten path of the well-worn map generally looks something like this: go to the highest-ranked school, follow orders, don't make waves, strive for the highest marks so that you can be accepted into the next highest-ranked school, where you will again strive for the highest marks and accomplishments—academic, athletic, and social—so that you can be accepted into the next highest-ranked school, where you will again strive for the highest marks and more accomplishments so that you can graduate with the highest possible honors which will land you a job with the highest-ranked company, with the largest paycheck and the highest-ranking title...so that you can buy the biggest, newest carriage full of bells and whistles, and the biggest castle to fill with the most bright, shiny objects, impressing all you meet...and along the way, all these "things" will land you the hand of The Princess or The Prince, and you will together make a few perfect children and give them all the twinkling things money can buy, and pass on to them The Map inside The Box. And you'll be anointed a success. And life will be perfect. And you'll live Happily Ever After. The End. You get the picture. "The Fairytale Picture."

The Map is a blueprint for creating The Fairytale Picture of The Prince and The Princess skipping happily ever after into the sunset with birds chirping, bunnies hopping, and music playing. The perfect world. The envy of all. The Map you were given may have looked slightly different than this, but it was a map of what others had decided was safe and noble to walk. The problem is, The Map doesn't work for many, if not most, of us.

Many of us are not born for the limiting confines of The Box, and the narrow path this Map navigates. We get pulled off-step, out of The Flow, lost in the weeds. The shoe pinches. And few people along the way ever offer a different Map, or a variety of different shoes. Or even a suggestion that there really is no Map for an authentic life.

Steve Jobs, pioneer of the personal computer revolution, visionary, and cofounder of one of the world's largest technology companies—Apple, urged, "Don't be trapped by dogma—which is living with the results of other people's thinking."[1] And Joseph Campbell cautioned, "If the path before you is clear, it's probably someone else's path. If you can see your path laid out in front of you step by step, you know it's not your path. Your own path you make with every step you take. That's why it's your path."[2]

Your Path most likely flows outside The Box. Yet, venturing outside The Box to forge through uncharted territory can feel daunting, overwhelming, even terrifying at times. Akin to feeling your way along in the dark. But here's the deal that perhaps no one has ever mentioned to you: everyone is feeling their way along in the dark. Everyone. Not even those in The Box with The Map have a crystal ball. Not even those famous who have flowed outside The Box to live their authentic, blissful life—like Oprah Winfrey and Steve Jobs—have a crystal ball. We are all, each and every one, feeling our way along in the dark, step by step.

None of us have life all figured out. And none of us possibly could because life is unpredictable, impermanent, and in constant evolution. No one can predict the future. No one. It twists and turns and morphs and evolves in unexpected ways, based on a glut of uncontrollable influences. Curveballs are thrown—economies crash, pandemics emerge, loved ones get sick or die, accidents happen. Strokes of luck appear—the new friend or love walks in, the unexpected gift arrives, the investment takes off, the tide turns. Life is a mysterious unfolding before our eyes, for each and every one of us, regardless of whether we use The Map or choose to walk our own Path. If we knew what lies ahead, we would miss out on the exhilaration of this wild ride, called Life.

4 | SOURCE

Imagine walking down to the ocean's edge with an empty plastic ziplock baggie—a biodegradable ziplock baggie. Imagine wading into the water, dipping the baggie in, filling it up, zipping it shut, and then tossing it back into the ocean. The water in the baggie is still the ocean water, it now just has a baggie around it.

The baggie full of water represents you. The ocean represents your Source. The ocean water now contained in the baggie is still part of the ocean. Much like you, your Soul, now contained in a human body, is still part of Source. When that biodegradable baggie disintegrates, the water will blend back into the ocean. Just as you —your atoms and awareness—will blend back into Source when your human body disintegrates. The first law of thermodynamics: "energy can be neither created nor destroyed, only transferred or exchanged from one form to another."[1]

"The universal doctrine teaches that all the visible structures of the world ... are the effects of a ubiquitous power out of which they rise, which supports and fills them during their manifestation, and back into which they must ultimately dissolve. This is the power known to science as energy, to the Melanesians as mana, to the Sioux Indians as Wokanda, the Hindus as Shakti, and the Christians as the power of God,"[2] explained Joseph Campbell.

And, just as the baggie full of water—a visible structure—will ebb and flow with the tides and currents of the ocean—an invisible power, your spirit ebbs and flows with the tides and currents of Source—the ubiquitous power. You feel a pull into The Flow, the same as the baggie of water feels a pull into the tides and currents of the ocean. Your pull is felt as longings, discontents, dreams, and desires. The Source of which you are made is pulling you. If you resist the pull, you will feel the exhausting suffering of struggle. If you surrender to the pull, you will easily drift along with the current of Source, like the Little Being in the story, who let go. You will fly. You will walk on the moving sidewalk.

We are conditioned to think that we are separate and alone, and must forge our life with individual will power. However, ultimately, we are not a human being having a spiritual experience, we are a spiritual being enjoying a human experience. We are divine. Our individual Soul is part of the one Source. We forget our divinity. We forget that we are a soulful being. We think we are only a human, an ego, a personality self.

What grew you from a microscopic egg and sperm into the person you are now? How did your heart begin beating and know to continue beating? What breathes you? Source. We are Source enjoying a human experience. We are each a drop in the great ocean. Thích Nhất Hạnh, who was one of the great spiritual teachers of the world, a Vietnamese Zen Buddhist monk, peace activist, and who was nominated for a Nobel Peace Prize by his friend Martin Luther King, Jr., described it simply this way: "Enlightenment for a wave is the moment the wave realizes it is water."[3]

The American planetary scientist, and astrophysicist Carl Sagan reported, "The nitrogen in our DNA, the calcium in our teeth, the iron in our blood, the carbon in our apple pies were made in the interiors of collapsing stars. We are made of starstuff."[4]

Planetary scientist and stardust expert Dr. Ashley King confirmed, "It is totally 100% true: nearly all the elements in the human body were made in a star and many have come through several supernovas."[5] You are made of the stuff of exploding stars. The Universe is not outside of you. You are the Universe. "I searched for God and found only myself. I searched for myself and found only God,"[6] realized Rumi.

A German physicist named Max Planck won the Nobel Prize in Physics for his work on the atom. Planck wanted to know what was the glue which holds the human body together. So he put the body under a microscope. He saw that the skin and bones, muscles and organs, are all composed of cells. He put the cells under the microscope and saw that all cells are created from a collection of atoms. He put the atoms under the microscope and he saw nothing. He saw nothing holding the atoms together. They appeared to be floating in space. There was no "glue."

Near the end of his life, at 86 years of age, he said this: "As a man who has devoted his whole life to the most clear-headed science, to the study of matter, I can tell you as a result of my research about atoms this much: there is no matter as such. All matter originates and exists only by virtue of a force which brings the particle of an atom to vibration and holds this most minute solar system of the atom together. We must assume behind this force the existence of a conscious and intelligent spirit. This spirit is the matrix of all matter."[7]

You are a collection of atoms vibrating in space, originating and existing only by virtue of a force—the conscious and intelligent Source. All of your atoms are floating in the same great ocean with all the atoms of everything else—animals, plants, stars, planets, galaxies. This is how we are all connected. We are all a collection of atoms floating, and vibrating, in the same ocean. You are Source experiencing humanness. "It is through life that one is to experience the spirit and communicate the spirit and live the spirit,"[8] explained Joseph Campbell.

Alan Wilson Watts, the British philosopher who interpreted Buddhism, Taoism, and Hinduism, taught it this way: "Every one of us is an aperture through which the whole Cosmos looks out. You see, it's as if you had a light covered with a black ball. And in this ball were pinholes. And each pinhole is an aperture through which the light comes out. So in that way, every one of us is actually a pinhole through which the fundamental light that is the existence itself looks out."[9] Like one of those "Lite-Brite" children's toys. Different colored pegs are arranged on a board in the foreground, lit by one lightbulb in the background. We are each a peg, lit by the same, one light.

Oprah Winfrey also shared, "If you ask me what is the secret to my success, it is because I understand that there is a power greater than myself, that rules my life. And in life, if you can be still long enough in all of your endeavors—the good times, the hard times—to connect yourself to the source, I call it 'God,' you can call it whatever you want to—the force, nature, Allah, the power—if you can connect yourself to the source and allow the energy that is your personality, your life force, to be connected to the greater force, anything is possible for you. I am proof of that. I think that my life, the fact that I was born where I was born, and the time that I was, and have been able to do what I have done speaks to the possibility. Not that I am special, but that it could be done. Hold the highest, grandest vision for yourself."[10]

"Because you are alive," offered Thích Nhất Hạnh, "anything is possible."[11] You are unlimited because you are made from the unlimited ocean of Source. You are by your very nature, unlimited Source, and therefore have access to infinite awareness.

But we forget our omniscience while being conditioned to rely on our limited human brain.

The word "namasté" is a Sanskrit word, the great spiritual language of the world, which acknowledges the divinity of each individual. It means, "I honor the place in you in which the entire universe dwells. I honor that place in you of love, of truth, of light, and of peace. When you are in that place in you, and I am in that place in me, we are one." When you are aligned with that place of oneness—Source—your human abilities expand, and anything is possible.

Ram Dass, the American-born Richard Alpert, Stanford-educated Harvard professor turned spiritual teacher, and author of the influential book *Be Here Now*, realized, "The final awakening is the embracing of the darkness into the light. That means embracing our humanity as well as our divinity. What we go from is being born into our humanity, sleep walking for a long time, until we awaken and start to taste our divinity. And then [we] want to finally get free. We see as long as we grab at our divinity and push away our humanity we aren't free. If you want to be free, you can't push away anything. You have to embrace it all. It's all 'God.'"[12] Embrace both your humanity and your divinity. It's all Source.

5 | EGO

Our "humanity" is our human perspective, our ego. It's our sense of self, self-esteem, or self-importance. It's the part of us that says, "I am." I am a woman. I am a man. I am a body. I am a worker. I am a title. I am a recipient of a degree or an award. I am the owner of a bank account. I am a relationship status. I am an ethnicity. I am a citizen. I am a political affiliation, etc. All these are your characteristics but they are not completely "you." They are the labels, the walls, the facade, the baggie, all of which house the you, which is your Soul—Source.

The problem with the ego is not the fact that we have one. In fact, it is absolutely necessary and useful to have an ego in order for our Soul to operate on earth as a human. The problems arise when the ego believes it to be the Self, the Soul, Source. While the ego is vital in helping us to navigate our earthly experience, identification with the ego causes delusion, and needless suffering.

The suffering arises when we make choices in alignment with the ego's need to create the superficial Fairytale Picture, and hang on to that. You get the job, and buy the big house, and fill it with all the stuff, and you buy the fancy car, etc. You get the ring, you have the children. You have the expectations of how life should go, and what the picture should look like, and what the outcomes should be. And in the process you sacrifice your soul's deep longings, as well as your mental, emotional, and physical balance and health.

The Fairytale Picture becomes the golden handcuffs which enslave your heart and Soul. You relinquish your power. Your ego holds your Self captive, outside of The Flow.

A big key to staying in The Flow is to become aware of when your ego is leading. There can be only one driver. When your ego is navigating or calling the shots, that means your Soul is not. With awareness, you can kindly invite your ego to move comfortably into the copilot seat, and enjoy the ride. Shift your awareness from aligning with the ego to aligning with your Soul, over and over again. It is a constant practice. This is so important, it's worth repeating: to stay in The Flow, become aware of when your ego is leading, and consistently choose to follow your Soul. When in The Flow, your ego is your copilot, and your Soul is the pilot. Your ego is the rudder to the sail of your Soul. They operate together. They are teammates, collaborators. We can embrace both our humanity and our divinity as Source.

To realign with and follow your Soul, let go of attachment to the ego, external validation, The Picture, and certainty. In doing so, you slip out of the golden handcuffs and sink back into your sacred Center, realigned with your fundamental energy—Source, your inner compass—and flow from there. The artist Georgia O'Keeffe, recognized as the "Mother of American modernism," said, "I have already settled it for myself so flattery and criticism go down the same drain, and I am quite free."[1]

"To live a truly whole and fundamentally fulfilled life, we must," as the political commentator and writer David Brooks realized, "fall through the ego, and ask, 'What do my heart and soul want?'"[2] Fall through your ego into that deeper space, beneath your carefully crafted, superficial facade, down into the core of your heart and Soul. There you will find your inspiration, your compass, your connection to the well of Source.

6 | PERFECTION

Perfection is an illusion of the ego. Stephen Hawking, the British scientist, who performed groundbreaking work in physics, stated, "One of the basic rules of the universe is that nothing is perfect. Perfection simply doesn't exist. Without imperfection neither you nor I would exist."[1]

The definition of perfection is the absence of all flaws or defects. We are all born imperfect. We are each a mixed bag of strengths and weaknesses, pros and cons. Our "flaws" and "defects" are the marks which give our humanness character, depth, texture, and richness.

Karla MacLaren, a social science researcher, and author of *The Language of Emotions*, has found that perfection is a sign you have lost your flow.[2] Wow. Trying to be perfect is one sure, fast way off track, out of The Flow.

Ironically, most of us are taught to strive for perfection—to "get our ducks in a row." Only then, when achieving perfection, have we succeeded in validating our self-worth and attaining happiness. We can then finally sit back, breathe a sigh of relief, and coast comfortably through our perfect Fairytale Picture life, knowing we've done a fine job, stamped with approval. We get attached to an image of perfection—The Picture. And when life can't match that image, we are then caught in the emotions triggered by a perceived failure.

For years I tried to get my ducks in a row and achieve The Picture so that I could feel worthy and happy. I went to the great schools, earned the requisite degree, landed the glamorous job, and looked for my Prince. Yet, try as I might, my ducks would never stay in a row. I wasn't married young to a "catch," climbing the corporate ladder, and producing babies in a designer home for a picture-perfect photograph full of forced smiles to send out on a holiday card. My picture was never "perfect." And, not only did I not feel worthy and happy, I felt miserable, even suicidal at times. Until I learned to let go of The Picture and align with *my* truth, my bliss.

Here's a fact: we will never get our ducks in a neat and tidy, perfect little row, and then skip happily ever after into the sunset with the perfect soundtrack playing in the background. Because ducks don't stay in a neat and tidy little row. They move. They are organic. Even if you could get them in a row, they wouldn't and couldn't stay there. Everything in life is flowing, vibrating, pulsating in a pattern of expansion and contraction—your breathing, your heartbeat, the oceans and rivers, the seasons and planets and galaxies, sound, light. All move in waves. Nothing is static, everything moves; some faster, some slower. Everything is energy in constant motion. Even a stone or a mountain. This awareness can bring great relief, allowing us to let go of the unrealistic notion of ducks in a row, a fixed destination, a perfect life, and accept the natural flow. "Perfection is static, and I am in full progress,"[3] reflected Anaïs Nin.

Pema Chödrön, the New York City-born Deirdre Blomfield-Brown, Berkeley-educated, ordained Tibetan Buddhist nun, divorcée, mother, grandmother, author, and teacher realized, "Things don't really get solved. They come together and they fall apart. Then they come together and they fall apart. Then they come together and fall apart again. It's just like that. The healing comes from letting there be room for all of this to happen: room for grief, for relief, for misery, for joy."[4]

Forget about working to get your ducks in a row. Life is very much like surfing waves. Life goes up and down for all of us. Coming together and falling apart. This constant expansion and contraction is inherent in life and requires a continual balancing act. But it doesn't have to be hard, and it should be fun—staying loose, grounded, and flexible, like a skilled surfer. So, hop on your surfboard and enjoy the ride.

Anna Quindlen, the American writer and winner of the Pulitzer Prize for Commentary, said, "The thing that is really hard, and really amazing, is giving up on being perfect and beginning the work of becoming yourself."[5] Joseph Campbell clarified, "The privilege of a lifetime is to be who you are."[6]

Yoyo Ma, considered to be the greatest cellist in the world, was a child prodigy performing from the age of four. He attended the renowned performing arts conservatory The Juilliard School, graduated from Harvard University, and performed as a soloist with orchestras around the world. "At one point," he recalled, "I had the audacity to think I could play a perfect concert. I was in the middle of a concert and I realized everything's going perfectly well. And I was bored out of my mind. That was the moment that I made a fateful decision that I was actually going to devote my life to human expression versus human perfection.... I've been playing the cello for over 60 years, so I should be getting it right by now. However, is that what I'm trying to do? Am I trying to get it right or am I trying to find something? ... what creates magical moments. That magic is something living. And to me, that's the essence of what I try to do in music—transmitting something so it lives in somebody else."[7]

7 | SUCCESS

If perfection isn't success, then what is "success" anyway? The Map in The Box and the ego define success in terms of numbers. Generally, the bigger, the better—get into the highest-ranked school, get the highest marks in class, score the highest points on tests and in games, land a job with the highest-ranked company, earn a paycheck with the biggest number, buy a home with the most square feet, have the biggest bank account balance, have the most possessions, have the most followers, be as famous and popular and wealthy as possible. *Then* you've achieved success.

The idea of "success" for many people revolves around the escalating acquisition of money, possessions, and positions. This is the ego in action. The fact is, many people who follow The Map inside The Box and achieve the big numbers, possessions, and positions, wake up one day and don't feel as happy or successful as they thought they should. One can appear to be successful based on society's and the ego's definition but still feel something is missing. Until you define what success means to you on an intrinsic level, you will be chasing empty accomplishments. You'll be experiencing outer riches, yet inner poverty.

Jim Carrey, the actor and comedian, who personally experienced great fame, fortune, possessions and positions, reported, "I've often said that I wished people could realize all their dreams of wealth and fame, so they could see that it's not where you'll find your sense of completion. I think everybody should get rich and famous and do everything they ever dreamed of so they can see that it's not the answer. I don't believe in icons. I don't believe in personalities. I believe that peace lies beyond personality and disguise, beyond the red S on your chest that makes bullets bounce off. I believe that it's deeper than that."[1]

Deeper than fame and fortune. Joseph Campbell summarized, "People say that what we're all seeking is a meaning for life. I don't think that's what we're seeking. I think that what we're seeking is an experience of being alive, so that our life experiences on the purely physical plane will have resonances with our own innermost being and reality, so that we actually feel the rapture of being alive."[2]

We long to feel the rapture, the magic, the exhilaration of being alive, deep in our innermost being. To feel this, simply fall through your superficial ego into your deep well of bliss—the umbilical to Source. The ego reaches outside for what can only be found inside. The outlet to bliss lies inside. Plug your awareness into your bliss.

There is absolutely nothing inherently wrong with posses-sions and positions, acknowledgment and validation. They are simply the sweet, appreciated byproducts—treasures—found on our authentic Path when following our inner compass. Although, to make possessions and positions the goal is like putting the cart before the horse and wondering why we aren't getting to the land of fulfillment.

The American yoga teacher, and activist Seane Corn taught, "Teaching tip #2...Don't do it for the money. Don't do it for the celebrity. Don't do it for the validation you're sure to receive. Do it because the moment you open your mouth, or place your hands on someone's body, you feel, without a doubt, the undeniable presence of spirit lingering between each breath and moving within your touch. Teach to serve. Teach to share. Teach because it is your art, your communication with the world within, beyond, seen and unreal. If the money, success and validation come, know that is its own deep, and temporal, yoga for you to navigate. Don't let it distract you from being truly of service to God, each other and this planet, as well as being a conduit for healing and love."[3]

Many accomplished people who have staked their flag into the top of the mountain agree that the pinnacle of success in life isn't the stardom or things or esteem. It isn't the money or the stuff or the title. It's absolutely the amount of joy that you feel. The bliss. The magic. The rapture. The exhilaration. And that comes from being in alignment with who you really are. So that your thoughts, words, actions, and creations stem from the real you—a Soul, flowing from Source.

Barnard-educated and reformed perfectionist Anna Quindlen also shared that when she "quit the *New York Times* to be a full-time mother, the voices of the world said I was nuts. When I quit it again to be a full-time novelist, they said I was nuts again. But I am not nuts. I am happy. I am successful on my own terms. Because if your success is not on your own terms, if it looks good to the world but does not feel good in your heart, it is not success at all."[4]

We are taught to create The Picture, but often The Picture doesn't *feel* good. Our life *must* feel good in our own heart if we are to ultimately feel satisfied and successful. To live a truly fulfilling life, "'What will they think of me?,' must be put aside for bliss," noted Joseph Campbell.[5]

Sir Richard Branson, whose dyslexia caused him to drop out of school at age 15, said, "I think if somebody sets out to make a lot of money … they most likely won't succeed. Earning enough money in the year to pay the bills is important. Making a fortune from being successful is not important. I've never taken things like clothes or cars or material things very seriously at all. People, family, all those sorts of things are really important."[6]

You lose yourself—your way, your Path, your connection to Source—when you try to find your worth on the outside. Seeking external validation in money, grades, titles, approval ratings, material things, etc., is normal, programmed, egoic, human behavior. But the truth is that we can never feel completely successful without the experience of being in alignment with our Center. Period. There is no substitute for it. Although external sources appear to be promising replacements, the cup of satisfaction, joy, and completion fills up from an internal spring. Deeply resonant fulfillment is very much an inside job. Success is an inside job. It's a feeling, not a picture.

"Being successful at almost anything means having a passion for it. If you see somebody with even reasonable intelligence and a terrific passion for what they do, things are gonna happen,"[7] proclaimed Warren Buffett, the American businessman, investor, and one of the world's wealthiest people. Steve Jobs shared, "I'm convinced that the only thing that kept me going (during the devastating period after being fired from Apple) is that I loved what I did. You've got to find what you love. And that is as true for work as it is for your lovers. Your work is going to fill a large part of your life, and the only way to be truly satisfied is to do what you believe is great work. And the only way to do great work is to love what you do."[8] Oprah suggested, "Forget about the fast lane. If you really want to fly, just harness your power to your passion. Honor your calling. Everybody has one. Trust your heart and success will come to you."[9] Ralph Waldo Emerson, the 19th-century American philosopher whose core belief was the unlimited potential of each person, wrote, "Nothing great was ever achieved without enthusiasm."[10] Feelings of passion, love, and enthusiasm, are the signs of authentic, intrinsic success.

Be completely aware of how you *feel*, and which altars you lay your time, treasure, and talent on. Make a conscious choice to not sacrifice or abandon your heart, body, mind, or Soul for the Fairy-tale Picture, or the things, people, and forces which deplete rather than nourish you. The authentic Path defines success as feelings of joy, passion, love, and enthusiasm, which don't stem from all those extrinsic riches. Reject any notion of success other than what resonates as success on *your* internal gauge of deep inner fulfillment.

"Whether you succeed or not is irrelevant, there is no such thing. Making your unknown known is the important thing, and keeping the unknown always beyond you,"[11] said Georgia O'Keeffe. She was describing the fulfilling process of feeling her way along in the dark—mapless, one step at a time, navigating with her inner compass—as her unknown became known, and continually watching her Path unfold mysteriously in front of her.

If you feel unfulfilled, even when things look successful on the outside and "good on paper," or you feel that "something's not quite right" even though you can't put your finger on it, maybe you have veered away from your umbilical to Source, your bliss. "At any moment, you have a choice, that either leads you closer to your spirit or further away from it,"[12] clarified Thích Nhất Hạnh. Commit to making choices, every moment, in alignment with your heart and Soul, passion and enthusiasm.

Failure. Does the very word make you cringe and recoil? This reaction is simply our conditioning. What is failure? "Failure is part of the journey to success....Failure is not the opposite of success, it's a stepping-stone to success,"[1] shared Arianna Huffington, mother, divorcée, businesswoman, co-founder of *The Huffington Post*, founder of Thrive Global, gubernatorial candidate, author, named to *Time Magazine*'s list of the world's 100 most influential people, and the *Forbes* Most Powerful Women list.

"Failure is not the opposite of success, it's part of success. When you realize that," interpreted the writer Alyssa Satara, "you free yourself from the fear of failure. In life, failure is inevitable. And the best leaders learn from their failure. They use it as a tool to become successful."[2]

"There is only one thing that makes a dream impossible to achieve: the fear of failure,"[3] wrote Paulo Coelho, the Brazilian novelist, who, at the age of 17 was committed by his parents to a mental institution from which he escaped three times before being released at the age of 20; dropped out of law school; traveled the world; was arrested for "subversive" activities and tortured by the ruling military government; and after 40 years of age left a lucrative career as a songwriter to pursue full-time his dream of writing.

Failure is inevitable. Life is one big experiment for all of us. Remember, no one has the crystal ball. Failure is not a death knell to be avoided at all costs, it's simply defined as the lack of desired outcome. That's all it is: things not working out the way you wanted them to. Failure is the raw material of wisdom.

However, the word "failure" holds a lot of emotional charge. It's very triggering. As if it's a reflection of our innate inadequacy. The word "failure" has been programmed into our minds with a negative connotation. No one likes to fail because we associate failure with humiliation and pain. A dark smudge on the shiny facade of our ego's carefully crafted projection. However, if we are to flow along our authentic Path, we must reprogram our definition of failure. If we view a failure as an embarrassing reflection of our personal inadequacy, or as a setback to be avoided at all cost, failure will be debilitating. If, on the other hand, we can see failure as the wonderful lesson that it is, we can move forward wiser and stronger. "Mistakes," suggested the American author Richard Bach, "call them unexpected learning experiences."[4]

"The world has so many lessons to teach you," shared Oprah Winfrey. "I consider the world, this earth, to be like a school and our life the classrooms. And sometimes here in the 'planet earth school' the lessons often come dressed up as detours or roadblocks. And sometimes as full-blown crises. And the secret I've learned to getting ahead is being open to the lessons—lessons from the grandest university of all—that is the universe itself."[5]

Thomas Edison was a prolific American inventor with over 1,000 patents in his name. When asked how he persevered through 10,000 failures as he searched for the formula for the electric lightbulb, he replied, "I have not failed. I've just found 10,000 ways that won't work."[6] Edison viewed failure as valuable feedback, a gift to use. Each time he tried an idea and it didn't work, he learned the lesson to take forward, stronger and wiser. 10,000 times.

"The 'uh-oh' moments are worth cherishing just as much as 'ah-ha' moments. Mistakes, failures, embarrassments and disappointments are a necessary component of growing wise. We can learn *more* from our not-so-good experiences than we can learn from our good ones."[7] reported Sonia Sotomayor, who was born amidst poverty to Puerto Rican immigrants, raised in public housing by a single mother after her father's death, learned to utilize her "uh-oh" moments, went on to be awarded the Pyne Prize—the highest honor awarded a Princeton undergraduate, became editor of the Yale Law Journal, and eventually the first Latina US Supreme Court Justice.

If we deny the 'uh-oh' moments—try to sweep them under the rug, numb ourselves from the experience, or wish they never happened—we squander an immensely valuable lesson. We turn away from a door of opportunity that has opened for us. We turn down an invitation to something greater.

Every failure, no matter how bad it seems, holds within it a lesson of some kind. And that lesson is a blessing. The goal is to find it. When you replace "why is this torturing me" with "what pearl of wisdom is this offering me" everything shifts. Practice shifting your perspective on failure to feedback. Value all feedback, and use it.

Oprah Winfrey advised, "Turn your wounds into wisdom. You will be wounded many times in your life. You'll make mistakes. Some people will call them failures but I have learned that failure is really God's way of saying, 'Excuse me, you're moving in the wrong direction.' It's just an experience, just an experience."[8]

Failure is simply another part of life. There is no way around it. There are stories upon stories of people who have not let failure stop them in their tracks. They extracted the lesson, they leveraged the blessing.

J.K. Rowling, the British writer best known for the fantasy series *Harry Potter,* which became the best selling book series in history, said, "You might never fail on the scale I did, but some failure in life is inevitable. It is impossible to live without failing at something, unless you live so cautiously that you might as well not have lived at all. In which case, you fail by default."[9]

Miles Davis, the American jazz musician, who is among the most influential and acclaimed figures in the history of jazz and 20th-century music, said, "When you hit a wrong note, it's the next note that makes it good or bad."[10]

We all hit wrong notes in our life. Consistently. Many wrong notes. No way around it. Your whole life is one big experiment to the end. What matters most is the next note—how gracefully you recover. When you stumble, make it part of the dance.

"Where you stumble and fall, there you will find your treasure,"[11] taught Joseph Campbell. When you fall, pick up the treasure—learn something to take forward with you—feel thankful for the pearl of wisdom, and use it. That's what mistakes are for.

"What defines us is how well we rise after falling," said an anonymous wise soul. When we use failure—those things that didn't go the way we wanted—as an opportunity to learn, we can then grow, improve, and evolve. We can make a conscious choice to not be a prisoner of our past. It was just a lesson, not a life sentence. We can choose instead to become the builder of our future. "I am not what happened to me. I am what I choose to become,"[12] suggested Carl Jung. Another wise soul said, "If you could erase all the mistakes of your past, you would also erase all the wisdom of your present. Remember the lesson, not the disappointment." Experience is what you get when you don't get what you want. Turn your wounds into wisdom.

Nelson Mandela, the South African anti-apartheid revolutionary, whose challenges are well-documented, was arrested by a white government in 1962 and sentenced to life imprisonment. From inside the prison walls, he spent 27 challenging and prolific years persevering to help lead his revolution, until finally being released and democratically elected the first black president of the country which imprisoned him. After all of his trials and tribulations, he reportedly said, "Do not judge me by my success, judge me by how many times I fell down and got back up again."[13] A classic Japanese proverb says, "Fall seven times, get up eight." Often life knocks us down. We have the choice to either stay down or get back up, now wiser, and move on. Success is not the absence of failure, it's the ability to use it.

9 | CHALLENGE

Failure, challenges, and problems are all part of life. Sometimes life does knock us down. Sometimes life will throw a curveball, or pull the rug out from under us, or blindside us. We are often taught to believe that if we simply follow The Map inside The Box, coloring carefully inside the lines, we will avoid challenges, and our ducks will stay in their neat and tidy little row, and we'll be successful and feel happy, but here's the absolute truth: the downs of life go with the ups. There are no ups without the downs. They are inextricably interwoven.

Ancient Chinese philosophy created a very clear and beautiful symbol for this balance. It's called the "yin and yang," meaning positive and negative. It looks like two fish intertwined, one black, one white, and represents "dualism"—equal and opposite *complementary* forces present in all of nature, interconnected, and interdependent. The opposites give rise to each other as they interrelate. Everything in life has an equal and opposite counterpart. For example, hot and cold exist together, as do up and down, wet and dry, inhale and exhale, sunrise and sunset, etc. The light exists with the dark. Ease cannot exist without challenge.

As much as we strive to create only easy, good, pleasant lives, we cannot escape the other half—the challenges, the uncomfortable, the unpleasant. The opposites are always present in order to create a necessary balancing tension between these two polarities. Therefore, accepting and working with these inherent challenges helps us to navigate our Path with greater balance, ease, and strength.

Anne Bradstreet, the 17th-century English poet, observed, "If we had no winter, the spring would not be so pleasant: if we did not sometimes taste of adversity, prosperity would not be so welcome."[1] The American entertainer Dolly Parton agreed, "If you want the rainbow, you gotta put up with the rain."[2] And Martin Luther King, Jr., the American Baptist minister and activist who became the most visible spokesperson and leader in the American civil rights movement, offered, "Only when it's dark enough can you see the stars."[3]

"We have the tendency to run away from suffering and to look for happiness," reflected Thích Nhất Hạnh. "But, in fact, if you have not suffered, you have no chance to experience real happiness."[4] Challenge and adversity aren't something we can avoid. They are half of life. They don't need to debilitate, destroy, or derail us. They can be seen as a natural part of life, and viewed as gifts in their own right. "Life's challenges are not supposed to paralyze you, they're supposed to help you discover who you are,"[5] encouraged Bernice Johnson Reagon, a civil rights song leader.

When speaking about challenges, Joseph Campbell, author of *The Hero's Journey*, had a lot to say. "Opportunities to find deeper powers within ourselves come when life seems most challenging."[6] The great news is that at those times when life is most challenging, you can be certain that you will meet the depths of your inner power and resolve. This is a phenomenal gift.

J.K. Rowling had her own story of challenge. She was a divorced, poor, suicidal, single mother living in grim public housing when she wrote the first *Harry Potter* book. "Rock bottom became the solid foundation on which I rebuilt my life,"[7] she shared. Often our lives need to fall apart so that something greater can fall together. What the caterpillar calls the end of the world, the butterfly calls the beginning.

"If you want to become full, let yourself be empty. If you want to be reborn, let yourself die. If you want to be given everything, give everything up,"[8] taught Lao Tzu, the ancient Chinese philosopher. Paulo Coelho related, "When I had nothing to lose, I had everything. When I stopped being who I am, I found myself."[9]

The mythologist John Bucher, when describing "The Hero's Journey," wrote, "That every ending brought forth new beginnings, that every death brought forth resurrection and new life. From death comes life. From what has passed, a new story emerges."[10] From compost comes fruit. "No mud, no lotus," is a classic Zen proverb. When you feel like life is burying you, remember, you are a seed. The seed must be buried to open and grow, the fruit must be picked to be eaten, the berry must be crushed to make jam. Every act of creation is first an act of destruction. New life requires old death.

Adversity, challenges, trouble, obstacles, failure, heartache, loss always carry a seed of a greater opportunity. It is a gift for you to find, a present for you to unwrap. Nelson Mandela, through all of his challenges and struggles, proclaimed, "I never lose. I either win, or I learn."[11] How powerful is that statement? Win the lesson every time you are challenged so that you move forward wiser and stronger. This is how we grow and evolve. "Out of suffering have emerged the strongest souls; the most massive characters are seared with scars,"[11] observed Khalil Gibran, the 19th-century Lebanese-American writer.

Seek to discover the gift within the challenge. "The pearl is in the oyster. And the oyster is at the bottom of the sea. Dive deep,"[12] wrote Kabir Das, the 15th-century Indian poet.

10 | PAIN

Another challenge, and natural part of life, is pain. Yet, many of us spend our lives trying to avoid pain at all costs. This effort at avoidance and control creates even more pain, which is called suffering. "Pain is inevitable, but suffering is optional," is a classic Buddhist proverb. The intention to avoid pain is one of the biggest factors that pulls us off our Path. Yet we often make choices with this intent. We stand in The Box, trying to look down the road and calculate which step to take in order to avoid pain, and then make our move from there. We must realize that pain is unavoidable, learn to deal with it, and avoid suffering.

We lose jobs, homes, money, things. We get sick, have accidents, and make mistakes. Loved ones die or leave. Pandemics and Great Depressions and Recessions emerge. Wars, earthquakes, tsunamis, tornados, hurricanes, famine, floods, fires. This is life. And it can be painful. "Pain is part of there being a world at all...I will participate in the game. It is a wonderful, wonderful opera, except that it hurts,"[1] perceived Joseph Campbell.

Here's a fact: everyone experiences pain and discomfort. Those in The Box, and those in The Flow. Trying to cling to The Box to avoid pain is futile. You may as well let go, live your truth, and learn how to navigate pain.

The key to navigating pain is to not struggle against it. Give up trying to push it away, give up trying to cling to and grasp for pleasure instead. When pain comes, let it roll on through, like river water flowing over your open palms. "This too shall pass." It's the resistance which creates the suffering. Trying to push away pain is like trying to push away river water. It's futile. Put your energy into allowing it to be present, and allowing it to flow on down the river.

Flowing outside The Box isn't a cake walk. Residing inside The Box isn't a cake walk, either. There is no cake walk, regardless of the path you choose. Yet it is far more exhilarating and fulfilling to stay aligned with your inner compass no matter where it leads, knowing that when you meet pain, you can watch it move on through.

We cannot run away from our problems, our pain. "Wherever you go, there you are," goes the old adage. You want to live an authentic life? You want to feel like you are walking a Path true to yourself, and feel the magic and exhilaration and rapture of being alive? Get comfortable with pain and discomfort. Allow it to exist in your world without being hijacked by it. Joseph Campbell suggested, "Find a place inside where there's joy, and the joy will burn out the pain."[2]

Know this: when life is going your way, nice and comfortable, there isn't much impetus to grow. Growth occurs at the edges of your comfort zone. Stepping outside The Box and encountering a challenge doesn't mean you are failing. Our authentic Path includes intense challenges at times. You can either choose to shrink from life's inherent challenges and exert immense effort trying to huddle safely inside The Box—clinging to the bottom of the fast-moving river, like the Little Being—or you can embrace it, and enjoy navigating the waves of challenge like a skilled surfer, and flow outside The Box. This is ultimately your choice.

The British writer Vivienne Green observed, "Life isn't about waiting for the storm to pass. It's about learning how to dance in the rain."[3] "You can't stop the waves, but you can learn to surf,"[4] experienced Jon Kabat-Zinn, the creator of Mindfulness-Based Stress Reduction program—MBSR. "Ships are safe in harbor. But that's not what ships are built for," said some wise soul. And, "A calm sea never made a skilled sailor," goes another adage. Live your life, dance in the rain, surf the waves, navigate your ship. Enjoy the ride!

The author Richard Kiyosaki wrote, "Life is the best teacher of all. Most of the time, life does not talk to you. It just sort of pushes you around. Each push is life saying, 'Wake up, there is something I want you to learn.' If you learn life's lessons, you will do well. If not, life will just continue to push you around. Life pushes all of us around. Some people give up and others fight. A few learn the lesson and move on. They welcome life pushing them around. To these few people, it means they need and want to learn something. They learn and move on."[5]

When life goes your way, say thank you and celebrate. When life challenges you, say thank you and celebrate the lesson. No regrets in life, just lessons learned to become wiser and stronger and fuller and more evolved and vibrant. "Life doesn't get easier or more forgiving, we get stronger and more resilient,"[6] observed the author Steve Maraboli. If you chose.

11 | PERSEVERANCE

Which leads to perseverance. Perseverance is to persist in doing something despite challenge, difficulty, delay, or setback to achieve success, and is a requirement on your Path because we all at times encounter difficulty and delay in realizing our dreams. Setbacks are simply another natural part of life. It is your choice whether to give up or to persist. As you persist, and grow, and evolve on your Path, your dreams may evolve and change, too, and that's okay. Or your dreams may persist for years and decades, so stick with them, stay true to them, honor the call of your heart.

Albert Camus, the French philosopher, and writer, who at the age of 44 became the second-youngest recipient in history to win the Nobel Prize in Literature, was born into poverty, never knew his father who died fighting in WWI, suffered tuberculosis as a teenager, was living in Paris in his late 20s when the Germans marched in during WWII, tried to flee, ended up joining the French Resistance, and realized, "Sometimes carrying on, just carrying on, is the superhuman achievement."[1]

It's been reported that at age 23, Oprah was fired from her first reporting job. At age 27, Vincent Van Gogh failed as a missionary and decided to go to art school. At age 28, J.K. Rowling was a suicidal single parent living on welfare. At age 30, Harrison Ford was a carpenter. At 30, Martha Stewart was a stockbroker. At 37, Ang Lee was a stay-at-home-dad working odd jobs. Julia Child released her first cookbook at 39, and landed her own cooking show at 51. Vera Wang failed to make the Olympic figure-skating team, didn't get the editor-in-chief position at *Vogue*, and designed her first dress at 40. Stan Lee didn't release his first big comic book until he was 40. Alan Rickman gave up his graphic design career to pursue acting at 42. Samuel L. Jackson didn't get his first movie role until he was 46. Morgan Freeman landed his first major movie role at 52. Kathryn Bigelow only reached international success at age 57. Grandma Moses didn't begin her painting career until age 76. And Louise Bourgeois didn't become a known artist until she was 78.[2]

"If you haven't found it yet, keep looking. And don't settle. As with all matters of the heart, you'll know when you find it,"[3] related Steve Jobs, who dropped out of college his freshman year. Two years later he traveled through India studying Zen Buddhism and seeking enlightenment. And two years later cofounded the company, Apple. Nine years later he was forced out of the company—fired—after a long power struggle with the company's board and CEO, and went on to cofound other ventures, including Pixar, before returning as CEO to revive the failing Apple, 21 years after co-founding it.

Every act of creation looks like a mess in the middle. Think about it. Baking a cake. Painting a picture. Building a home. Life is inherently messy. Allow for the mess. Embrace the creative process. It's only in hindsight that we can see the full unfolded creation. And really that doesn't happen until we take our last breath.

Every person who has ever stepped out of The Box and into The Flow has encountered challenges, setbacks, frustration. We can choose to shrink and cower in fear, or we can choose to use these forces to learn, grow, move forward stronger, and persevere. Anything worth having is worth working for.

Sometimes we can feel frozen with overwhelm when navigating our Path. It's as though we are standing at the base of a mountain, looking up at the peak, and wondering how in the world we will ever get there. The prospect can be so daunting that we feel defeated even before beginning. One step at a time gets you up the mountain. Keep putting one foot in front of the other. One step, one moment, one breath at a time. "The journey of a thousand miles begins with a single step,"[4] assured Lao Tzu. "You don't have to see the whole staircase, just take the first step,"[5] encouraged Martin Luther King, Jr.

Brené Brown, whose 2010 TED Talk "The Power of Vulnerability" is one of the most viewed talks in the world, is a mother, wife, research professor at the University of Houston, a visiting professor at The University of Texas, an author of multiple books, and a podcast host. She discovered, "I've never achieved a single thing in my career or life comfortably."[6]

Diana Nyad, a distance swimmer, had a dream. She wanted to swim from Florida to Cuba. In 1978, at the age of 28, having set many distance records as a competitive swimmer, she attempted to swim from Havana to Key West. But due to strong winds and 8-foot swells pushing her off-course, she had to stop. Yet her dream persisted.

Thirty-two years later, in 2010, at the age of 60, she began training for a second attempt at the 60-hour, 103-mile swim. When asked about her motivation, she said, "Because I'd like to prove to the other 60-year-olds that it is never too late to start your dreams."[7] In August 2010, the scheduled swim was canceled, due to bad weather. Still, her dream persisted.

She rescheduled for July 2011, but a record stretch of high winds and dropping water temperatures prevented her from attempting. In August 2011, some 33 years after her first attempt, Nyad tried again. And again she was thwarted—after 29 hours in the water—with shoulder pain, a flare-up of asthma, and encountering strong currents and winds that pushed her miles off course. Still, her dream persisted.

In September 2011, she began a third attempt but stopped after 41 hours and roughly 67 miles through the 103-mile course, due to respiratory distress caused by jellyfish and Portuguese man-of-war stings, plus currents pushing her off course. Still, her dream persisted.

Her fourth attempt in August 2012, after having covered more distance than her three previous attempts, ended prematurely, because of two storms and nine jellyfish stings. And, still, her dream persisted.

Finally, in 2013, on her fifth attempt, Diana Nyad, at age 64, became the first person confirmed to swim 110 miles from Havana, Cuba, to Key West, Florida.

Diana Nyad's dream to swim from Florida to Cuba is a lesson in failure and perseverance. After many, many years and many, many setbacks, she did not give up. She persevered. She stayed true to her dream—to that pull in her heart, to the call of her soul, to the longing of Source expressing through her. Each time she failed, she used the lessons to move forward wiser and stronger. "Life is 10% what happens to you, and 90% how you respond to it," goes the adage. On her fifth and final attempt, she adopted the mantra: "Find a way."[8]

What defines us is how well we rise after falling. We all fall down at times. We all meet resistance. There are always options. Giving up is one option. Choosing to glean the pearl of wisdom from the challenge, and find a way to persevere is another. Find a way. Intend to find a way. "What lies behind us and what lies before us are tiny matters compared to what lies within us,"[9] observed Ralph Waldo Emerson.

"The will is so undefinable and can push you so far beyond," shared Nyad. "I've had sports scientists, the best of them, write me and say, 'I'm sorry to tell you, this is humanly impossible.' And I write back and say to them, 'You have no idea then. You're just doing your little studies on what the heart can do, and what the lungs can do. I'm talking to you about what the spirit can do, and that's not measurable.' The spirit is larger than the body. Find a way."[10]

Don't let others' limited minds limit your unlimited Soul. Don't give your power away. If you close a door in your mind, you also close a door in your life. Keep the doors in your mind wide open in order to open as many doors as possible in your life. And always remember that the only thing limiting your limitless Soul is the mental constraints placed on it by the limited mind.

Diana Nyad had both the necessary physical ability and, more importantly, the positive mental stamina. "Sports physiology studies have shown that in 'extreme' marathon-type activities, mental determination is a more important factor than the physical energy of youth."[11] Your life Path can be considered an extreme marathon-type activity. It's a Heroine's or Hero's Journey. Mental determination will always be a more important factor than any challenge you face. Therefore, learning to work with the mind is a prerequisite for successfully navigating your unique, authentic, one-of-a-kind, dream-come-true Path.

12 | THE MIND

Every thought in your mind is like a pebble in a pond, rippling out to create every word you speak, every action you take, and everything you create. All are first a thought. Therefore, the first step is to work with your mind. It's absolutely necessary to make working with your mind a lifelong commitment because what you choose to hold in your mind creates your life. And you cannot have a positive, exhilarating, fulfilling life with a negative, narrow mind.

Our mind is much like a computer—programmable. From birth onward, our mind is being programmed by parents, teachers, peers, family, community, the media, and other influences. We generally absorb these programs, perspectives, and beliefs without question, and dismiss anything lying outside of them. Many of us run our whole lives on autopilot based on the limiting programs we've been given.

It is vital to become aware of the programs in your mind and continually upgrade or delete them, as necessary. Just like your personal computer, as information advances, some programs become obsolete and need to be replaced. Yet many of us are operating our whole life on the obsolete programs installed many years ago at a very young age, and are not even aware that we are being run by these mindsets or the fact that we have the power to change them.

According to Yoga, a 5,000-year-old physical, mental, and spiritual practice originating in India, both the root of life's problems and their solutions lie in the mind. In one of the foundational texts of classical Yoga philosophy, *The Yoga Sūtras of Patañjali*, compiled some 2,000 years ago, the very first 4 aphorisms, or sayings, state that the teaching of yoga is first and foremost, "to still the patterns of consciousness. Then pure awareness can abide in its very nature. Otherwise awareness takes itself to be the patterns of consciousness."

In other words, be aware of what you are thinking. Your beliefs, opinions, and judgements are your "patterns of consciousness." With practice and skill you can notice those limiting beliefs, and choose, instead, to remain open-minded, and curious. Thus allowing your awareness to "abide in its very nature" of limitless possibility.

Our mind often jumps to conclusions, makes assumptions, and spins tall tales based on our programming. "In the absence of data we will always make up stories. That's human nature,"[1] reported Brené Brown. Our mind will fill in the blanks. And, FYI, because evolution has hard-wired a "negativity bias"[2] into our brain for survival, those assumptions, conclusions, and tales will most often be negative. If we believe those made-up, negative stories, we then speak and act from fiction, rather than fact. And this is problematic, first and foremost because the track of our authentic Path is made of truth. If you pause and inquire for the absolute truth of a thought, deciding if it's worth harboring or replacing, you then have the ability to proceed only from a foundation of truth. And you stay on track.

The mind, being programmable, will believe what you tell it. A lot of the pain we are dealing with is really only thoughts. Monitor your thoughts, assumptions, and stories, harbor the truth and replace the rest with more authentic and empowering thoughts. "Be mindful of your self-talk. It is your conversation with the Universe,"[3] taught Taoist Master David James Lees. Feed your mind with inspiration and encouragement. Engage in an empowering, generative conversation with the Universe.

"Achieving control of your thoughts so that your thoughts don't control you can be a super-power for many people,"[4] reported Dr. Vernon Williams, neurologist and founding director of the Center for Sports Neurology and Pain Medicine at Cedars-Sinai Kerlan-Jobe Institute.

Monitoring your mind, continually, for limiting beliefs is hugely important work. This exercise is helpful: when you notice a belief popping up, write it down. A belief can sound like, "He *always* does that; those people are like this; I'm *horrible* at math; she *can't* cook; I *always* [fill in the blank]; they *never* [fill in the blank]; I *can't* [fill in the blank]. [Fill in the blank] is *not* possible." Make a list. You might be amazed at all the limiting beliefs currently installed in your programming and how they have narrowed your options and created the life you now have. Next to each entry on the list that you've made, write down a new belief—a replacement that opens your mind and allows more doors in your life to open. "He *sometimes* does that; I *am* sufficient with the math that I use in my daily life; she *can* cook, and I sometimes don't enjoy the taste of her cooking; I *sometimes* [fill in the blank]; it *may* be possible if I explore it." Moving forward, anytime you notice a particular belief popping up, pause, and replace it with the new belief you've written. In essence, reprogramming your brain. And opening up doors of opportunity in your life.

To continually grow and blossom into our fullest potential, we must reprogram our minds throughout our lives. To paraphrase the American futurist Alvin Toffler, "the illiterate of the 21st century will not be those who cannot read and write, but those who cannot learn, unlearn and relearn."[5] Become the observer. Pay attention to the thoughts you harbor and then decide if those thoughts are creating the life your heart desires. If not, change your thoughts. Unlearn and relearn. Evolve your mindset. Read new books. Meet new people. Learn. Grow. Switch it up. Upgrade your programs.

What a relief it is to realize that we are not our thoughts. We are simply the observer of our thoughts. We are "pure awareness." The witness. "Leave your front door and your back door open. Allow your thoughts to come and go. Just don't serve them tea,"[6] instructed the Zen monk Shunryu Suzuki Roshi.

A classic Zen story tells of Nan-in, a Japanese master. A university professor came to see Nan-in, inquiring about learning Zen. While Nan-in poured his visitor a cup of tea, the professor talked incessantly—proudly displaying his vast knowledge. As he talked, Nan-in kept pouring until the tea was overflowing the cup. The professor watched until he could take it no longer, and snapped, "It is overfull. No more will go in!" To which Nan-in calmly replied, "Like this cup, you are full of your own opinions and speculations. How can I show you Zen unless you first empty your cup?"

"Shoshin" is a Japanese word from Zen Buddhism, meaning "beginner's mind," and refers to having an open-minded attitude, one without preconceived notions, when studying a subject, even at an advanced level, akin to a beginner. Shoshin applies to life. In order to stay in The Flow, we must be willing to keep our minds open to possibilities, clear of limiting beliefs and patterns of consciousness.

"I decided to start anew—to strip away what I had been taught, to accept as true my own thinking,"[7] shared Georgia O'Keeffe, the innovative American modernist painter who is celebrated as one of the greatest artists of all time.

"My story," said Richard Branson, "(and the story of Virgin) is a tale of big dreams. The odds have often been stacked against me, but by not limiting myself to what I have been told to be true, I have been able to make the impossible possible."[8]

Reflecting on a difficult period of his life, Steve Jobs stated, "I didn't see it then, but it turned out that getting fired from Apple was the best thing that could have ever happened to me. The heaviness of being successful was replaced by the lightness of being a beginner again, less sure about everything. It freed me to enter one of the most creative periods of my life."[9]

And, the Spanish artist Pablo Picasso, regarded as one of the most influential artists of the 20th century, was reported to have said, "It took me four years to paint like Raphael, but a lifetime to paint like a child."[10] He spent most of his life trying to unlearn the formal training he had learned—to open the doors in his mind which had been closed—and access the pure energy of creation that children express.

When your mind is full of programmed thoughts, beliefs, and opinions, or lost in memories, future projections, negative assumptions, or stories, you inhibit your greatest potential. When you establish the habit of becoming aware, you can "stand guard at the portal of the mind"—discerning which thoughts to harbor and which to release and replace. You can use your mind, as the wonderful tool it is, to serve your heart and Soul.

"One's mind may be likened to a garden," penned the British writer James Allen, "which may be intelligently cultivated or allowed to run wild; but whether cultivated or neglected, it must, and will, bring forth. If no useful seeds are put into it, then an abundance of useless weeds will fall therein; and continue to produce their kind."[11] "Your mind is a garden. Your thoughts are the seeds. You can grow flowers. Or you can grow weeds," goes the saying. "In our consciousness, there are many negative seeds and also many positive seeds," taught Thích Nhất Hạnh. "The practice is to avoid watering the negative seeds, and identify and water the positive seeds every day."[12]

Just as it is important for physical health to monitor what we feed our body, it is equally important for mental health to monitor what we feed our mind. If we feed our body toxic food we become physically ill. If we feed our mind toxic thoughts, we become mentally ill.

When a destructive thought—such as judgment, resentment, or revenge—enters your mind, notice it, and replace it with a constructive thought—such as compassion, generosity, or under-standing. We are all alchemists. We possess the ability to turn our destructive thoughts into constructive thoughts simply through awareness and choice. This is our personal power of alchemy. We choose to water the positive seeds. This takes awareness and practice.

Maria Forleo, an American entrepreneur, author, and named by Oprah Winfrey as a thought leader for the next generation, cautioned, "Make no mistake my friends, what we say to ourselves in the privacy of our own minds matters. It drives our behavior which drives our destiny which shapes our world."[13] You live your life inside of your head. Make sure it's a nice place to be.

We all have an inner critic living inside our head who is quick to judge, condemn, and jump to negative assumptions. I call mine Darla. "Dueling Darla." The key is to know when Darla is talking, and not let her hijack my thoughts, words, and actions. My awareness has a relationship with Darla, and can say, "Okay, Darla, I hear you, thank you, that's enough. Now please take a back seat." Befriend your inner critic, and never let it in the driver's seat. Ever. Otherwise you will allow your inner critic to lead you through an inauthentic life, running you off the rails by speaking and acting in ways that create a world in which you don't enjoy living.

Be extremely mindful of which seeds have been planted in your mind, and which you water with your attention and focus. "Energy flows where attention goes." Do you water the seeds which support yourself and others—the seeds of joy, empathy, benevolence? Or do you water the seeds which destroy yourself and others—the seeds of fear, animosity, bitterness? Do you water the seeds which are in alignment with your heart's desire? Or do you water the seeds which are in alignment with your ego's desires? You can either focus on the positive, lift yourself up, and fly, or focus on the negative, crash, and burn. This is ultimately your choice.

This is not to stick your head in the sand or deny the truth of what is. This is to step into your authentic power by choosing your perspective. The Roman emperor and philosopher Marcus Aurelius, who lived almost 2,000 years ago, said, "Very little is needed to make a happy life; it is all within yourself, in your way of thinking. The happiness of your life depends upon the quality of your thoughts. Everything we hear is an opinion, not a fact. Everything we see is a perspective, not the truth. You have power over your mind, not outside events. Realize this, and you will find strength."[14]

We all want a happy life. Yet most of us are taught that happiness is something that is external, and visited upon us when we can achieve, or buy, or produce a particular something—the grades, the job, the money, the mate, the house, the car, the body, the award, etc. And then, only then—when we get those ducks in a row—will we be happy.

What is now known, from much research across cultures, is that happiness is a choice, not a result. It's not a feeling that magically materializes when life goes our way. We *choose* to be happy. It's in our way of thinking. No matter what is happening. Nothing will make us happy until we choose to be happy. No person can make us happy unless we decide to be happy. Our happiness will not come to us. It can only come from us. It's generated internally.

Helen Gurley Brown, the American publisher and editor-in-chief for 32 years of the women's fashion and entertainment magazine *Cosmopolitan*, who lived a glamorous, jet-setting life with her film and theater producer husband of 50+ years, realized, "The happiest people I know are not those who are the most beautiful, rich, or famous. The happiest people I see are simply those who stay cheerful and try to cheer up others while getting through their own bad stuff."[15]

If happiness is a choice, as happiness researchers around the globe have discovered, and luminaries have espoused for centuries, then all it takes to feel happiness is a shift in perspective, a shift in the way you look at things.

"Our notions of happiness entrap us," taught Thích Nhất Hạnh. "We forget that they are just ideas. Our idea of happiness can actually prevent us from being happy. We fail to see the opportunity for joy that is right in front of us when we are caught in a belief that happiness should take a particular form. Our ideas of happiness may be the main obstacle keeping us from true happiness."[16] Be aware of which particular thoughts create your unhappiness—those patterns of consciousness. With awareness, the opportunity to experience happiness is always available in the present moment through a shift in your perspective.

Once during a moment of darkness and struggle I thought to myself, "Is this all there is?" At lightning speed, a "knowing" arose—Source speaking, "Yes! This *is* all there is." And in my mind flashed images of my child's face, family and friends, ladybugs on leaves, blue skies, and sunsets, birds chirping in majestic trees, canyons and snow-capped mountains and babbling brooks, ocean waves, dancing and beautiful music and delicious cupcakes, and kisses, and hugs, and the scent of flowers and fragrance. The images kept coming, and I realized, yes, this *is* ALL there is. And it is quite magnificent. If I spend my time focused on lack, I will miss the overflowing abundance of wealth, as it is right now, in each and every moment.

Our unhappiness stems not from the objective situation but our subjective interpretation and thoughts about it. "Change the way you look at things," goes the saying, "and the things you look at change." This is one of the basic wisdom teachings which has been passed down through the centuries: perspective = reality.

With awareness, we have the power to shift our perspective at any moment. Every thought is your choice. If you are asleep at the wheel—running on autopilot, lost in your patterns of consciousness—your thoughts will be running the show, and may run you off the rails of your authentic Path. When you "wake up," and become aware, you can choose more empowering thoughts which keep you in alignment with your heart's calling, your bliss—Source.

The Sanskrit word for awake is buddha. "The Buddha," as the story goes, was simply a guy named Siddhartha Gautama who was born in the area of present-day Nepal and lived in India about 2,500 years ago. He was given the nickname "Buddha" because he was awake to, and not run by, the patterns of his consciousness. Apparently his awakened state was quite inspirational to many, and they copied his method, thus forming the practice of Buddhism— the practice of becoming awake.

Gay Hendricks, PhD, a Stanford-educated psychologist, teacher, and writer, illuminated something called the "upper limit problem." The upper limit problem basically means that "if you don't know it's okay to feel good all the time, you'll do something to mess up when things are going well."[17] Apparently we all have an inner thermostat of how happy we can be and how much joy we can let into our life. This setting is partially innate—some of us are born happy-go-lucky, while others carry the weight of the world on our shoulders—and partially programmed into us at an early age by conditioning. If something good happens in our life to raise our thermostat setting beyond its upper limit—moving us out of our comfort zone, an unconscious program will be triggered to bring the setting back down and move us back into that comfort zone. The antidote to solving the upper limit problem is to become *aware* of when this is happening, and make a conscious *choice* to "expand in love and joy."

Brené Brown described it this way: "Joy is deeply vulnerable. We're afraid to lean into joy because something might rip it away and we'll get sucker punched by disappointment or pain. But there's a way to stay in joy: When we feel that quiver of vulnerability, instead of dress-rehearsing tragedy and waiting for the other shoe to drop, let that shudder be a reminder to practice gratitude."[18] We can reprogram our thermostat setting higher and higher by embracing joy and practicing gratitude.

Gratitude is the energy which immediately transforms any challenge or anguish on your Path into appreciation and adventure. Studies have shown that feelings of gratitude release feel-good hormones in the brain, such as serotonin, dopamine, and endorphins. Feelings of gratitude actually change your brain chemistry, pain is alleviated, and you feel uplifted. Habitually focusing on gratitude in any situation—shifting your perspective from negativity to gratitude—will help you flow. Cultivating "an attitude of gratitude," moment by moment, is one of the greatest ways to blossom into your fullest potential and enjoy your adventure. Attitude is the difference between agony and adventure.

The American high diver Laura Wilkinson, when beginning, was told by a teacher that she was too old to start a new sport, and was later kicked off her high school team because the swim coach thought she was a "waste of space." Her dream persisted, and she persevered elsewhere to become a national club champion, and a two-time NCAA champion at the University of Texas before landing a spot on the 2000 US Olympic diving team. Going into the Olympic competition, she was an absolute underdog to the strong and intense Chinese competitors who were easily favored to win. As she stood on the Olympic high-dive platform with an injured right foot, ready to take her final dive, after having ascended through the competition, she paused and looked around. Looking down at the crowd, and seeing her loved ones there cheering her on, she calmly marinated in the moment with a sense of palpable gratitude so powerful that you could see it in her eyes and in her smile, and I could feel it in my own heart. She was flooded with gratitude. And then she dove. "In one of the most improbable diving competitions in Olympic history," exclaimed the announcer, on an "unbelievable night," Laura beat out the competition to win the gold. "That is what can happen," he continued, "when a person is so positive and has such a positive, optimistic outlook."[19] Gratitude is absolutely and instantaneously transformative. Its power cannot be overstated. Laura said, "I smile because I love what I do. I make a commitment before the competition to enjoy the experience however it turns out."[20] It's the journey, baby!

Oprah shared, "I have learned to appreciate living in the moment … I believe that if you can learn to focus on what you have, you will always see that the universe is abundant and you will have more. If you concentrate and focus in your life on what you don't have, you will never have enough. Be grateful…. What it will begin to do is to change your perspective of your day and your life."[21]

Your thoughts are like a pebble in a pond. They ripple out like waves to create your emotions. Your emotions ripple out like waves to create your physical sensations. If you want to shift your emotions, or your physical sensations, words, or deeds, switch up your thoughts. If you want to create something different in your life, switch up your thoughts. If you want to flow outside The Box, and live a blissful, exhilarating, fulfilling life, switch up your thoughts. Throw a different pebble in the pond.

13 | EMOTIONS

Emotions? Why talk about emotions when most of us are taught from birth to sweep them under the rug, stuff them down, suppress or numb them as quickly as possible? We are taught that emotions are a nuisance to be avoided at all costs, run from as fast as possible, and distracted from in any number of ways available. Do anything but feel them. And certainly don't express or discuss them.

We may therefore believe that emotions, if felt, will swallow us up, drown us, or hold us hostage forever. However, emotions are simply "energy in motion—e-motion." That's all they are. They are like waves which rise, crest, and fall away. We can no more hold on to an emotion than we can a wave of the ocean. "Feelings," taught Thích Nhất Hạnh, "come and go like clouds in a windy sky."[1]

While "toxic positivity" dismisses negative emotions and responds to distress with false reassurances rather than empathy, "healthy positivity" acknowledges all emotions, accepts whatever genuine feelings arise, and sits with them compassionately until the wave of energy has passed on its own.

Pema Chödrön suggested, "We don't have to attach so much meaning to what arises, and we also don't have to identify with our emotions so strongly. All we need to do is allow ourselves to experience the energy, and, in time, it will move through you."[2] Like a wave on the ocean, or a cloud in the sky, emotions come and go. They are not you. Anything that comes and goes is not you. You are the awareness observing the comings and goings.

Emotions are what make us a human, not a robot. Every human being on earth received, as a part of their "standard operating system," a full set of emotions. It's like a keyboard. Elation, joy, and ecstasy on one end, and rage, terror, and grief on the other end, with tones of happiness, contentment, anger, sadness, fear, etc., in between. Different things will trigger different emotions in each of us. For example, what triggers fear in me, may not trigger fear in you; what presses your sadness key may not press another's. Yet each of our lives is one continuous symphony of emotions, as one morphs into the next. If you watch small children as they laugh one moment and cry the next, followed by a scream of anger, you will witness this emotional flow. As babies and children, we are naturally in that flow until we are conditioned and numbed out of it. Until the walls of The Box are built up around us.

Just as you are not your thoughts, but the observer of your thoughts, you are also not your emotions. You are the observer of this flow of emotions rising, cresting, and falling away. You are pure awareness observing emotions being triggered by thoughts. You don't have to identify with them so strongly. As soon as you stop identifying with your emotions and begin to observe them, you are no longer blended with and tangled up in them. And this is when you can begin to utilize their wisdom.

Karla McLaren points out in her book, *The Language of Emotions*, that each emotion is a brilliant messenger offering valuable wisdom to help guide us skillfully on our Path. Which makes them important. And which makes learning to work with them an essential endeavor because if we don't learn to consciously use the wisdom of our emotions, we will be unconsciously driven by them. For example, we can consciously observe a surge of anger as a warning sign that one of our boundaries has been infringed upon, and work mindfully and constructively to secure the boundary, or we can unconsciously act out, with misdirected, and potentially harmful, words or actions.

We all have within us an active volcano. And for many of us that volcano has a hair trigger. Someone comes along, says or does something, and boom! The volcano erupts, and we go flying off like molten lava, speaking and acting in ways that are damaging. With awareness, we can notice when the volcano has been triggered, and choose to observe the sensations of the erupting volcano within, instead of acting out on it. When we place our focus on observing the inner sensations of the emotion, we shift out of the trajectory of its expression. With practice, we can become more skillful at feeling and identifying the initial subtle rumblings of a forming eruption, and catch ourselves before it is full blown.

If emotions stay unconscious, they control us. When we bring them into our awareness, we can harness them. McLaren elaborates that each emotion asks a question. For example, anger asks, "What must be protected? What must be restored?" Sadness asks, "What needs to be released?" And fear asks, "What action needs to be taken?" And so forth. Learn to listen to the language of your emotions. And answer their call.

Some people say, "Oh, I'm never afraid." In actuality, everyone feels the flow of the energy of fear from time to time. To be disconnected from it is a liability. While an energy is present, and until it moves through, we can glean its wisdom for guidance in our life. When fear asks, "What action needs to be taken?" maybe a speeding car is approaching, or an angry boss, or a story in the mind.

The energy of fear surges to signal that an action needs to be taken for our survival. To be numb to fear, or any emotion, is a detriment because it disallows you the use of the wisdom being offered. It puts you at a disadvantage on your Path.

South African psychologist Susan David, PhD, one of the world's leading management thinkers, and a Harvard Medical School psychologist, declared, "Tough emotions are part of our contract with life. You don't get to have a meaningful career or raise a family or leave the world a better place without stress and discomfort. Discomfort is the price of admission to a meaningful life."[3]

This is an important and valuable life lesson because tough emotions will consistently be present throughout our life. Fear, doubt, and worry are constant companions on our Path. Whether we stay inside The Box or flow outside, these emotions will be regular visitors. In fact, as soon as we begin to feel a pull outside The Box, and step to the edge of our comfort zone, fear, doubt, and worry will greet us. It is important to know this. There is no stepping to the edge of The Box without encountering these three allies. They stand guard there. Their job is to protect you, keep you safe, and alert you to potential danger, not to debilitate you. They have their own value.

These allies will speak up regularly as you walk your authentic Path. And sometimes they will be so loud that you will want to run straight back to the safe confines of The Box where life seems so much more predictable, comfortable, and easy. Recognize them when they speak up. Honor them by acknowledging any danger or threat. Consider their advice. Take any necessary action—jump away from the speeding car, communicate with the angry boss, or inquire for the truth of the story in your head. Thank these allies for their concern and wisdom. And then invite them to sit comfortably in the back seat, enjoying the ride. Take a deep breath, and proceed. Put another foot forward on a step in the direction of your inner compass. Never let fear, doubt, or worry lead, for they will run you back to The Box as fast as they can. Be led by your passion and the dreams in your heart.

"I was afraid," said the American singer, songwriter, and Grammy Award winner, India Arie. "I didn't know how to run my business. I was afraid. But I knew that I couldn't keep doing the same thing or I was going to be off the path of my destiny. And that's death. It's not even being alive if you're not doing what you are here to do."[4]

Georgia O'Keeffe, recognized as one of the greatest painters of all time, was born in a Wisconsin farmhouse to dairy farmers, led a colorful, unconventional life in the art world of New York City and the solitude of rural New Mexico, and passed away at the ripe old age of 98, shared, "I've been absolutely terrified every moment of my life, and I've never let it keep me from doing a single thing I wanted to do. I'm frightened all the time. But I never let it stop me."[5]

Amanda Gorman, the American National Youth Poet Laureate, born with a speech impediment and auditory processing disorder, and who, at the tender age of 22, stood before a global audience of millions to deliver the inauguration poem to the 46th president of the United States, said, "The truth is I almost declined to be the inaugural poet. Why? I was terrified. I was scared of failing ... I was also terrified on a physical level.... And then it struck me: Maybe being brave enough doesn't mean lessening my fear, but listening to it.... I'm a firm believer that often terror is trying to tell us of a force far greater than despair. In this way, I look at fear not as cowardice but as a call forward.... If you're alive, you're afraid. If you're not afraid, then you're not paying attention.... And yes, I still am terrified every day. Yet fear can be love trying its best in the dark. So do not fear your fear. Own it. Free it. This isn't a liberation that I or anyone can give you—it is a power you must look for, learn, love, lead, and locate for yourself."[6]

Susan David, PhD, who is also an Instructor in Psychology at Harvard University and the founder and co-director of the Institute of Coaching at McLean Hospital of Harvard Medical School, said in her TED talk titled "The gift and power of emotional courage": "Research now shows that radical acceptance of all of our emotions, including the messy and difficult ones, is the cornerstone of resilience, thriving, mental health, and true authentic happiness."[7] Wow. Stop the press. Can we pause and take that in? Want to be happy? Want to be healthy? Want to thrive? Accept all your emotions. Completely.

Accept them and do what? Thích Nhất Hạnh advised, "When an unpleasant feeling—physical or mental—arises, the wise one does not worry, complain, weep, pound one's chest, pull one's hair, torture one's body and mind, or faint. One calmly observes that feeling, and is aware that it is only a feeling. One knows that one is not the feeling, and one is not caught by the feeling. Therefore, the pain cannot bind him or her."[8]

By observing the uncomfortable sensations of emotions and allowing those sensations to be present without the need to avoid them in any way, we can become comfortable with discomfort. One way to do this is to describe to yourself the "nitty gritty" of the sensations. What does it feel like inside your body? A lump in the throat? Butterflies in the stomach? Tension? An exploding volcano? Heaviness? Heat? Color? Urge to run? We can also investigate, "What is it trying to communicate? What is its message? What gift is it offering?" When we develop a collaborative relationship with our emotions, we make friends with them, honoring them as teammates, and gratefully welcoming their brilliant wisdom to help us navigate our Path with greater clarity and strength.

When we can welcome our difficult emotions with the exact same acceptance we welcome our positive emotions, we can lead our lives in wholeness and transform our feelings of suffering into feelings of comfort. You alone get to decide how you feel. Outer circumstances are what they are. They are simply facts: he said this, she did that, this happened. But you get to decide how you'll interpret those facts, and therefore, how you feel inside. This is your power. You decide your thoughts, you decide your feelings.

14 | THE BODY

Thoughts trigger emotions, and emotions trigger physical sensations. The thought of a car speeding toward you triggers fear which triggers a racing heart, and sweaty palms. The thought of your loved one smiling triggers joy which triggers a burst of energy and a warmth in your heart. Physical sensations are the language of the physical body.

This physical body you have is amazing—really, really, amazing. It grew from the joining of a microscopic egg and sperm. How did this egg and sperm know how to merge? How did this embryo, the size of a grain of rice, know how to grow itself into a fully formed human being? And continue to repair and regenerate itself? It's mind-boggling. When you cut your finger, it heals. When you break a bone, it mends. Your body breathes you, and beats your heart. It digests your food and keeps your internal temperature stable. Your brain constantly makes new synapses. How does it know how to do everything, everything, everything it does? The body has its own intelligence.

You are not your body, just as you are not your thoughts and you are not your emotions. You are pure awareness which has the awesome privilege of inhabiting this amazing body for a finite period of time, and observing it. You are the Universe witnessing its creation. Your eyes are the Universe observing itself. Your ears are the Universe listening to itself. Your five senses are the Universe experiencing itself as human.

This body acts as a vehicle for your Soul to navigate the spectacular, green, watery earth for a brief period of time, and enjoy the miraculous experience of being human. Just as your body would put on the appropriate space suit—an "extravehicular mobility unit"—to travel to the moon, your awareness has put on the appropriate space suit—a human body—to travel to earth.

Your body is not only a "sacred temple" which houses your Soul, it is also an antenna for Source. Divine intelligence speaks to you as signals in the body—a gut instinct, an intuition, a knowing, a pull in the heart, a discontent, a deep longing, or desire, a "Yes, this feels right!" or a "No, you are moving in the wrong direction." You can feel your way along in the dark on your authentic Path simply by tuning into this antenna. Oprah advised, "Lesson 1: follow your feelings. If it feels right, move forward. If it doesn't feel right, don't do it."[1]

Your body is your greatest ally. Tune in. Truth registers in the body as a feeling. And dishonesty registers in the body, too, as a different feeling. You know the difference. You feel it. You know when something lights you up inside, when it lifts your spirits. And you know when something drags you down. You feel that, too. Stay tuned in to your body's feelings. They will guide you.

"The body is a sacred garment," noted the iconic American modern dancer and choreographer Martha Graham. "It's your first and last garment. It is what you enter life with and depart life with, and it should be treated with honor."[2]

Take good care of this sacred garment. Treat it with honor by feeding it pure and nourishing foods, giving it plenty of water and rest and exercise, and keeping it clean and balanced. Appreciate it. Acknowledge its wisdom and its service to your Soul. When you take care of your body, you keep the antenna clean, and your awareness can enjoy a clearer, faster connection with the guidance from Source.

Few things are of greater value than a well-working, good-feeling body. Your health is gold. If, in the pursuit to amass the markers of success, health is lost, as many people experience, what worth then are all the positions and possessions?

Your physical body, this sacred space suit, is the vehicle which allows you to be here and experience this truly astonishing life on earth. And your space suit is compostable. It has a shelf life. After you take your last breath, your body will disintegrate, and its atoms will disperse back into the universe, just as the bio-degradable baggie would disintegrate, and its water would disperse back into the ocean. Energy can neither be created or destroyed, only converted from one form to another.

15 | SOUL

Amidst the steady stream of bodily sensations, and amidst the steady stream of emotions constantly rising, cresting, and falling away, and amidst the steady stream of thoughts constantly flowing through your mind, lies your Soul—the fundamental you.

We all have a Soul. And we all have a shared Soul. Our Soul is the biodegradable baggie full of ocean water. Our shared Soul is the ocean of Source. You are a drop in the ocean. You are one piece of a whole jigsaw puzzle. You are a spark of one great light. Your spark of Divinity is not your body, or your thoughts, or your emotions. Your spark is pure awareness.

Through the natural process of conditioning, we forget this fact. We think we are only a human—our personality self, our ego, our body, our thoughts, our emotions, our circumstances. Our "awareness takes itself to be the patterns of consciousness." We think that we are our job title and relationship status, our education credentials and our accolades and awards, our bank account balance, our home or neighborhood, our country club, our nationality, our race, our religion, our physical appearance, our political affiliations. None of these, however, is the fundamental you. You are pure awareness—a limitless part of the infinite Universe—a Soul.

Yet we can spend an exhausting amount of time carefully grooming the sparkling facade of our personality ego which we project out into the world as "me." And get completely caught up by making choices in life based on how to best maintain that facade. This will pull us out of our authentic Flow. There is nothing that can pull you out of The Flow faster than aligning with your ego. We must remember that we are not that shining shell of our facade. We are the brilliant light, the Soul, which illuminates that shell.

To realign with your Soul, make choices guided by your heart, not your ego. Prioritize your relationship with your Soul as the greatest friendship and the most passionate love affair of your life.

16 | INTUITION

How do you toss aside The Map, venture to the edge of The Box, and enter The Flow? "Let yourself be silently drawn by the strange pull of what you truly love. It will not lead you astray." What is pulling you now? What are your longings, desires, and discontents? Cultivate that connection with your inner compass. You were born with an inner compass for navigating this uncharted territory. It's called your intuition, your gut instinct, inner wisdom, the call, the strange pull.

"Much of what I stumbled into by following my curiosity and intuition turned out to be priceless later on,"[1] shared Steve Jobs.

Intuition is defined as the ability to understand something immediately, without the need for conscious reasoning. We all have the ability to understand things without conscious reasoning, yet we have been conditioned to not trust anything that we cannot consciously reason. We want proof, measurable evidence, something solid to hold onto.

Source doesn't speak in reason, proof, or evidence. That's the realm of the mind. Source speaks in energy, goosebumps, flashes. "There is a little voice that doesn't use words. Listen."[2] wrote Rumi. The "voice" of Source is often ineffable—too great or extreme to be expressed or described in words. It's a feeling. And if we follow that feeling, we will be guided along our unique, authentic Path and, in the process, feel vibrantly alive, and realize our greatest potential. Oprah also shared, "I remember being four or five years old, I certainly couldn't articulate it, but it was a feeling, and a feeling that I allowed myself to follow."[3]

Utilizing the gift of your intuition requires tuning in to that immediate understanding, that little wordless voice, and trusting it. "Trust your gut. 'Does this feel right? Does this feel good?' Remember, the decision is ultimately yours alone to make,"[4] shared the broadcast journalist Barbara Walters who was a renowned trailblazer for women in the early, male-dominated, world of broadcasting. Trust those deep longings and desires. Trust your goosebumps. Intuition is felt in the body. It does not originate from the conscious, reasoning, thinking mind. Don't overthink. Don't overthink. Don't overthink. You know more than you think you know, way more. This information comes through your inner body antenna from the omniscient Source, not from the limited human mind.

Mary Morrissey, spiritual teacher, life coach, and mentor, put it this way: "Your intuition gives you access to massive amounts of information that your conscious, thinking mind simply does not have. If you listen only to your logical mind when trying to achieve goals, you'll follow the well-trodden path. If you get support from people who live from commonplace thinking, you'll continue to get the results you always have. Your intuition is a direct connection to the one universal mind, the infinite intelligence that is breathing you and living through you. Your intuition has the answers you seek and knows how to get you from where you are today … to where you want to be. All you have to do is restore your connection to your Intuition, and learn to listen!"[5] Intuition will reveal The Path to you. Learn to trust your intuition and walk that Path, step by step, moment by moment.

The story goes that the musician Taylor Swift was a mere thirteen years old when she received a coveted development deal with RCA records, but left after a year because she wanted to make the music she wanted to make, and not change to fit someone else's idea of what she should create. She stayed true to her heart's desire, her passion. By trusting her intuition, she had the strength to step away from a deal that her ego most likely desired. She moved on to become one of the most-awarded and best-selling music artists of all time, as well as a role model and inspiration for many. Had she abandoned her intuition—the guidance from Source—and stepped out of her Flow to align with others, she most certainly would not have achieved what she has achieved on her Path. Had she been aligned with her ego and the fruits she wanted to reap rather than aligned with her heart's longings, and intuition, she would be on a completely different path. It's remarkable that a 14-year-old girl would have the strength of Self to not be influenced and swayed by the "expert" adults in her life. It takes many of us years and years of maturity and waking up to our programming to get back in touch with our own inner voice, and grow the strength to resist the forces of others. And many of us never do.

Steve Jobs encouraged, "Don't let the noise of others' opinions drown out your own inner voice."[6] To hear your own inner voice—those higher intuitive promptings—clear your heart and mind of darkness. This isn't a one-time thing. It requires continual effort, like house cleaning, or bathing. Get into the habit of clearing your heart and mind by noticing when a negative or defeating thought arises, perhaps from your inner critic or programming, and don't harbor it. Instead, acknowledge it, and clear it out of your mind by replacing it with a positive, empowering thought aligned with your heart's desire.

Your inner voice is there to guide you. But you can't hear it in a loud and busy environment. When you notice yourself feeling bloated from the activity and noise of daily life, step back, take a pause, and get quiet. It is important to carve out quiet time in order to stay tuned in to your inner wisdom and promptings. Ram Dass offered, "People say, 'What should I do with my life?' The more interesting question is, 'How do I cultivate the quietness of my being, where what I should do with my life becomes apparent?'"[7]

Oprah advised, "If there is a moment when you're not sure which direction to head in or what to do, I want you to center yourself, get still, and ask, 'Who am I meant to be? What would that person be doing at that moment?' As you reflect on that, you'll begin to see glimpses of the path you're destined for."[8]

How do you not let the noise of others' opinions drown out your own inner voice? Get quiet, and reconnect with your inner voice. Take time out—sit with eyes closed, or take a walk in nature, or a solo bike ride—whatever you can do to allow your awareness some space, some stillness, and uninterrupted time to hear the whisper of Source. Clean, cook, chop wood. There are many ways to focus the mind and allow your awareness to "hear" your inner voice.

Ram Dass also offered this wisdom: "The quieter you become, the more you can hear."[1] And it's true. Silence isn't empty, it's full of answers.

When you become quiet, you can hear your mind speak. Your mind speaks in thoughts. As you bring more awareness to the thoughts continually flowing through your mind, you can see that you are not your thoughts, you are the observer of those thoughts. And, with cultivated awareness, you can begin to work with those thoughts, standing guard at the portal of your mind—consciously choosing which thoughts to harbor, and which thoughts to release and replace. Make it a habit to replace destructive thoughts—like criticism and cynicism—with constructive thoughts—like compassion and caring. Everything begins in thought—every word, every action, every creation. "Watch your thoughts, they become words. Watch your words, they become actions. Watch your actions, they become habits. Watch your habits, they become your character. Watch your character, it becomes your destiny," said some wise soul. When you become quiet, you can hear your thoughts creating your destiny. Both the roots of life's problems and their solutions lie in the mind. Choose your thoughts judiciously.

When you become quiet, you can hear your emotions speak. Each emotion is a brilliant messenger with valuable wisdom to share. Only by listening can you recieve that guidance offered to help navigate your Path with greater clarity, strength, and ease.

When you become quiet, you can hear your body speak. Your body speaks in sensations. And it's constantly sending signals to your awareness in an effort to help cultivate balance and maintain ease. It's your greatest partner in health. Disease, dis-ease, of any sort is simply a state of being out of ease, out of balance. At first the sensations are subtle, like a whisper—a painful sensation, a cough, an itch. If you do not listen, the sensations become stronger and louder, until they are so loud and so strong that they simply cannot be ignored—you pull a hamstring, succumb to a virus, grow a rash. Begin to listen to your body and honor its subtle whispers by responding appropriately, as soon as possible. In this way you will be an active partner in avoiding accidents, injury, and illness, thereby maintaining homeostasis.

When you become quiet, you can hear your heart speak. Your heart speaks in desires, dreams, and longings. Listen for the dreams calling out from deep within your heart. As the Oscar-winning actress Lupita Nyong'o discovered, "Dreaming...is a glimpse of the thing you want to do that would make you feel most alive. A dream is a portal to your purpose."[2] And, after all, we're here to feel the rapture and exhilaration of being alive. Bliss is the language of the heart. The dreams calling out from your heart are your Path. Oftentimes The Path deviates from the known, safe, and narrow path taught to us—The Map in The Box. But as Joseph Campbell highlighted, "If you can see your path laid out in front of you, step by step, you know it's not your path. It's probably someone else's. Your own path you make with every step you take. That's why it's your path."[3] Listen in and follow your heart, feel your way along one step at a time, one moment at a time.

When you become quiet, you can hear your Soul speak. Your Soul speaks in intuition. Gut instinct. It's guiding you on your Path. It's your internal GPS, your inner compass. When the noise from the outside world is blaring with messages of all perspectives, it is the voice of your Soul which guides you sure-footedly along. To hear it, you must listen. When your Soul speaks, it resonates as a knowing, truth, wisdom. You know it. This is your way. This is your Tao. Go with it.

"Moment after moment you should completely devote yourself to listening to your inner voice,"[4] instructed Shunryu Suzuki Roshi, Zen monk and teacher. When we get quiet and listen, we allow the pull of Source's tides to register in our field of awareness. This pause—the quiet, the stillness—balances out the action, and is the fertile ground from which ideas and directions spring.

"Silence is essential," encouraged Thích Nhất Hạnh, "We need silence, just as much as we need air, just as much as plants need light. If our minds are crowded with words and thoughts, there is no space for us."[5]

"We pray, God listens. We meditate, God speaks," goes the proverb. In other words, we pray, Source listens. We meditate, Source speaks.

Just as when we eat, we need time for digestion before eating again, as we move out into action in the world, we need time for processing before taking action again. Therefore, some sort of mental stillness is important for our balance. Otherwise, we become bloated with the activity of life. The pause is essential. It's the yin to the yang of activity. Just as the inhale is necessary for an exhale to follow, the pause is necessary for action to follow. In the stillness is where we reconnect with our inner guidance.

"Nobody can do anything 24/7," said Arianna Huffington to Oprah Winfrey. "There needs to be time, where, if you don't call it meditation, at least there is a stepping away from the work. You don't have to call it meditation; it can be 'prayer.'" Oprah agreed, "I call it 'being still.' Can you give yourself 5 minutes of stillness?" "It's that reconnecting with that place inside us," continued Arianna. "For me, for many years it was like a deserted garden that I started weeding and tending to. And when we connect with that place of wisdom, strength and understanding, everything becomes easier. And it's there; it's as close as our next breath. Disconnecting from our technology to reconnect with ourselves is absolutely essential for wisdom."[1]

By cultivating a pause in life, we create the opportunity to reconnect with our inner wisdom, and receive clear guidance on where to step next. Once we take that step, we must then pause again to receive information regarding where to step next. This way we step sure-footedly forward into our next action. And repeat. And repeat. And repeat. This is how to navigate an authentic Path.

Think of a shaken snow globe. Once it's set down, the shaken particles settle, and clarity emerges. When we become still, the same principle applies—the particles of our being settle, and we can see clearly our next step.

Stepping along our own Path with clarity, and connected to our inner wisdom, requires mindfulness. Mindfulness is defined as the ability to pay attention, with a sense of open-minded curiosity and lack of judgment, to whatever is happening in the present moment—a blue sky, a woman speaking, a horn honking, a bank account balance, an itch, a relationship status, etc. It is to adopt an objective observer perspective to all that is going on—becoming a witness—where life is viewed factually, and untainted by our subjective opinions, beliefs, and ideas.

When you objectively observe the conditions of the present moment, you are no longer on autopilot. Your awareness is un-tangled from the inner circumstances of thoughts, emotions, and physical sensations, as well as the outer circumstances perceived through the five senses. As the witness, you are simply observing these conditions, as if watching a movie on a screen. This vital quality of mindfulness—untangled, unoccupied—allows space, an opening, for you to receive your inner wisdom. Guidance from Source bubbles up into your awareness.

Mindfulness, and the ability to receive that guidance, is cultivated through a practice of meditation. Meditation is a technique that we humans have been employing formally for thousands of years. It is not a complicated spiritual practice or something esoteric.

It's a simple mental exercise, available to everyone. A mental exercise for training the mind in attention. The exercise is to focus your attention on a single point, and when your focus wanders off—as it naturally will when distracted by the endless stream of thoughts churning through your busy mind—return your focus to that single point. Over and over again. That's it. Focus on one point, and when your focus wanders off, return it back to the focal point.

Meditation is made up of the repeated focused mind and the wandering mind, just as the breath is made up of the repeated inhale and the exhale. This expansion and contraction changes the shape of the brain, just as the repetitive expansion and contraction of a "bicep curl" will change the shape of a bicep muscle. Your brain is malleable, like your muscles. When it's exercised, and changes shape, a whole domino of physiological effects occur, which create calm, clarity, and inspiration.

For thousands of years, the breath has been used as a traditional point of focus. Yet some meditations use an object or a word or phrase. The chosen point of focus doesn't matter as long as you return your focus to that single point, over and over again. The more this is practiced, the easier it is to observe thoughts and feelings in the moment. And then you can work with those. "Meditation," taught Thích Nhất Hạnh, "is not evasion; it is a serene encounter with reality."[2]

A friend of mine told me of a man who was a surgeon. And the surgeon described how when he was in surgery, his mind was so intensely and fully focused that he experienced a meditative state. There are many ways to become present—focusing our full, undivided attention on a single point in the present moment— working, walking, cooking, cleaning, singing, sewing, dancing, drawing, chopping wood, carrying water, etc. "There is more than one route to Rome."

When you sit down, close your eyes and draw your awareness inward—or meditate in any way—you are stepping off of the hamster wheel of the busy mind, with so many things vying for your attention, and stepping into a world where you can listen deeply to the core aspect of yourself, which is Source. When you drop down out of the busy mind, fall through the ego, and come into connection with the vast reservoir of who you actually are at a deeper level, you reconnect to the truth of who you are, a Soul. You are then able to observe the personality self in action—those frothy surface waves, the dazzling ego—from the seat of your Soul.

It is by coming into this sacred space of the soul that you let go of the false masks, the carefully groomed facade, the games and roles you play, and reconnect with your divinity, your omniscience. Here, you gain access to the inner wisdom of ideas, metaphors, stories, songs, dance, your renewal, and your direction in life.

"In meditating, meditate on your own divinity. The goal of life is to be a vehicle for something higher,"[3] suggested Joseph Campbell. Many notable people who have walked their own unique Path to realize their greatest dreams and fullest potential, becoming a vehicle for something higher, used regular meditation to help them access their deepest wisdom.

Steve Jobs described his meditation this way: "If you just sit and observe, you will see how restless your mind is. If you try to calm it, it only makes it worse, but over time it does calm, and when it does, there's room to hear more subtle things—that's when your intuition starts to blossom and you start to see things more clearly and be in the present more. Your mind just slows down, and you see a tremendous expanse in the moment. You see so much more than you could see before. It's a discipline; you have to practice it."[4]

Thomas Edison, who invented the incandescent light bulb, the motion picture camera, the film projector, the phonograph, and who held over 1,000 patents in his name, is reported to have used meditation to access his intuition and ideas. The story goes that he would sit in a chair, holding a rock in his hand, with a large tin bucket on the floor beneath. If he dozed off and fell asleep, the rock would fall, hit the bucket, and wake him up. He wanted to stay in that place between sleep and wake, where his mind was at rest and his awareness was open to greater possibilities. He would then get an idea, go tinker in his workshop, and test it out. If it didn't work, he would go back to his "meditation seat" until another idea came to him, and so on. This is how he came up with his inventions. They began as ideas which sprung from the deep reservoir of inner wisdom and connection to something larger than his limited human mind. He tapped into the "omniscient, universal field of intelligence." He was known to have astutely realized, "Ideas come from 'space.'"[5] Not "outer space," but inner space. Every idea is channeled by Source through the instrument of the body. Space, mental space, is needed to receive these ideas.

Oprah described her meditation this way: "Although I'm a big proponent of formal meditation—for the discipline, joy, and calm it brings—I'm moving into an even greater phase of being fully present all the time. It's a heightened state of being that lets whatever you're doing be your best life, from moment to astonishing moment."[6]

When the great meditation teacher Thích Nhất Hạnh was asked if he meditated every day, he replied, "Not only every day, but every moment. While drinking, while talking, while writing, while watering our garden. It's always possible to practice living in the here and the now. That is what we call meditation."[7]

It's certainly not required to retreat to a mountaintop cave or a designated meditation center for lengthy periods of time to practice in order to build the habit of mindfulness. There is more than one route to Rome. We can cultivate the basic habit of living in the here and now, fully embodied in this present moment, not lost on the hamster wheel of the busy mind, anytime and anywhere.

"The aim of all religious exercises is a psychological transformation. You can make up your own meditations and rites based on knowing, loving, and serving the deity—in caring for your children, doctoring drunks, or writing books. Any work whatsoever can be a meditation if you have the sense that everything is 'brahman' (Source)—the process, the doing, the thing that is being looked at, the one that is looking—everything,"[8] interpreted Joseph Campbell.

"The Soul loves to meditate, for in contact with the [Source] lies its greatest joy,"[9] said Yogananda, the Indian Hindu monk, and guru.

FORMAL MEDITATION TECHNIQUES:

*These meditation techniques can be done any time of
day, ideally for 10 minutes or more. One of the keys for
maintaining a practice is to do it at the same time every
day, and in the same, comfortable place,
free of major distraction.*

SITTING ON THE RIVER BANK:

In this practice, become comfortably seated, close your
eyes, and enjoy a few deep, full breaths. Imagine yourself
standing in an ankle-deep river. Then imagine yourself
stepping out of the river, up onto the riverbank, sitting
down comfortably, and peacefully watching the river
flow by. The river is a metaphor for all of your thoughts,
feelings, and physical sensations, as well as the circumstances of the moment—the people present, the things
and situations present: the fragrance you smell, your
health status, the city you live in, the home you live in,
the temperature of the air, the sounds you hear, etc. It's
all "the river." When you observe the river, you have created a space between your awareness and the river. And
in that space you can receive inner wisdom bubbling up
from Source into your awareness. Whenever you notice
that your focus has become tangled again—in thoughts,
emotions, or sensations, you've inadvertently stepped
back in the river. Step out of the river again and take
another seat on the riverbank. And repeat. And repeat.
And repeat.

~

SIT LIKE A MOUNTAIN:

In this practice, become comfortably seated, close your eyes, and enjoy a few deep, full breaths. Then, imagine yourself to be a mountain. Feel your foundation—whatever part of your body is touching the earth—feet, seat, legs—and allow it to sink down into the energy of gravity, growing heavy, grounded, and stable like the base of a mountain. From there, lift your spine up through the top of your head. The top of your head is the peak of your mountain. Everything below your belly button roots down, while everything above your belly button lifts up. Feel that sense of balance. Within that balance, allow your whole body to soften, relax, and rest. You are a restful mountain. From here, as a calm, stable, restful mountain, observe the clouds passing by. The clouds are a metaphor for your thoughts, emotions, physical sensations, and life circumstances in the present moment. As you observe the clouds from your mountain, you are not attached to them, and you can enjoy a feeling of grounded inner calm. And in the space between your awareness and all conditions of your human experience in the present moment, you can hear Source speak.

~

HEART FOCUS:

In this practice, become comfortably seated, close your eyes, and enjoy a few deep, full breaths. Then bring your awareness to your heart and ask, "Am I doing what I most want to be doing with my life? What would I love to be doing?" Whatever comes up, seize it before your mind snatches and dismisses it. Allow it to sit in the center of your consciousness for now. Listen, and take good notes. When your focus wanders off—captured by the random thoughts flowing through your mind: a sound outside the window; an uncomfortable emotion or sensation in the body—gently guide it back to the question.
And repeat.

~

BODY FOCUS:

In this practice, become comfortably seated, close your eyes, and enjoy a few deep, full breaths. Then bring your awareness to your body and ask it, "How are you doing? Tell me what I need to know or do in order to help you function best." Whatever comes up, seize it before your mind snatches and dismisses it. It could be an image or a thought, a metaphor or a hunch. Allow it to sit in the center of your consciousness for now. Listen, and take good notes. When your focus wanders off, captured by the random thoughts flowing through your mind, gently guide it back to the question.
And repeat.

~

19 | THE PATH

The Path, YOUR unique, authentic Path, is made one step at a time, in the moment. Each moment you are free to choose where to step next. Do you take a step from your mental programs—The Map inside The Box—or do you take a step from your inner guidance and intuition? Do you take a step based on your ego's desired outcome or do you take a step based on where your heart is guiding you? Do you take a step informed by your limited human mind or informed by the unlimited Universal Mind of Source? This is ultimately your choice.

Your Path is a journey through each moment. It's not about arriving at a destination. The Path is this present moment unfolding into the next. This present moment is where you are alive and vibrant. All else is memories, future projections, and stories. As the present moments string together like beads on a strand, your life Path is created. You cannot see The Path laid out in front of you. You can only see it laid out behind you. The unknown is ahead of you—an empty strand to fill with the beads of your choices in each present moment.

Your Path is not The Map you've inherited from your early caregivers, and it's also not a straight line from Point A to Point B. It's astonishing and spectacular and crooked, with twists and turns, and loops. It's a magical mystery ride. Even if you choose to stay inside The Box and follow The Map, your path is unpredictable because there is no way even The Map can anticipate the patches of overgrowth to tread, and fallen trees to hurdle, the earthquakes and storms, the dark nights and dark creatures jumping out and slithering toward you, which will test your strength and offer you wisdom, the lights which help to illuminate your Path and the friendly souls to warm your heart, the magical doors opening at just the right moment, and the treasures sprinkling down from the heavens. It's never a linear, smooth sail. You would be bored to tears if it were.

The exhilaration and magic of your personal journey is in taking those alluring forks calling your name, which pull you off the beaten path; exploring the mysterious caves which pique your curiosity; and diving deep into the dark to retrieve the pearl in the oyster. Even with fear, doubt, and worry along for the ride. Following your inner compass in the moment is what makes life true, interesting, and fun.

"Most [people] lead lives of quiet desperation,"[1] observed Henry David Thoreau. Instead, suggested the American writer Hunter S. Thompson, "Life should not be a journey to the grave with the intention of arriving safely in a pretty and well-preserved body, but rather to skid in broadside in a cloud of smoke, thoroughly used up, totally worn out, and loudly proclaiming 'Wow! What a Ride!'"[2] Which will you choose? The choice is completely yours. "The big question," suggested Joseph Campbell, "is whether you are going to be able to say a hearty yes to your adventure."[3]

To navigate The Path—your personal, extraordinary quest, not someone else's—through uncharted territory requires staying aligned with your "Center." Your umbilical to Source. Your Center is the balance point between the roots of your values and the wings of your heart's desires. Your values—the roots of your life—are what ground you. Your desires—the wings of your life—are what lift you up and help you fly. Get crystal clear about what you value most in life and what your heart's greatest desires are. It's important to know your roots and wings in order to continually make choices which are in alignment with these. Aligning with your truth keeps you on track. When you encounter difficulty and setback, as you most certainly will, return to that place of balance between your roots and wings, values and dreams. And begin again. And repeat. And repeat. And repeat.

It's been reported that when the space shuttle travels to the moon, it doesn't travel in a straight line. Its nose will veer off course a bit, but it will course correct in the direction of the moon, over and over again. Therefore, the shuttle's path to the moon is more of a zigzag. Similar to a car's path on the road.

This is also true of your life Path. You will continually veer off course because this is the nature of energy in motion. Think of walking a tightrope. Or drawing a straight line. You continually course correct as you go. "Keep your eye on the ball." Know your priorities. "At any moment," observed Thích Nhất Hạnh, "you have a choice that either leads you closer to your spirit or further from it."[4]

Your Center resides beneath the constant churning of thoughts through your busy mind—opinions, beliefs, judgments, resentments, grudges, fantasies—and beneath all of the emotions and physical sensations flowing through your body. It's the sacred core of your being, your Spirit. Return there and begin again. Again. And again.

"There's something inside you that knows when you're in the center, that knows when you're on the beam or off the beam. And if you get off the beam to earn money, you've lost your life.

And if you stay in the center and don't get any money, you still have your bliss,"[5] said Joseph Campbell. We fall off the beam when chasing the money, the approval, The Picture. And we can get back on the beam at any time by following our bliss.

Ask yourself, "What is my bliss? And what is the next best step in alignment with it?" Just as you can drive a car all the way from San Francisco to New York City in the dark because you have headlights showing you the next few feet, you can navigate your life Path "in the dark" because you have an inner light illuminating the next step. That inner light is your bliss. It's what lights you up inside. Follow that.

A surrendering must occur. Surrender. Does the very word make you shudder? What does surrender mean? Does it mean to give up? To be dominated? To surrender means to let go of aligning with the ego in order to follow your heart and bliss. Surrender your individual will and limited mind to the pull of Source. Surrender to The Flow. Go with the pull rather than oppose it. Walk on the moving sidewalk rather than walk up the down escalator. It doesn't always make sense to the limited mind, or the ego. Often it doesn't. And that's okay.

I remember vividly my own moment of surrender. It was at a particularly painful time in my life, when the struggle to hold The Fairytale Picture together had reached an excruciating tension. It was during The Great Recession. My coveted career had been imploding uncontrollably in the escalating avalanche of layoffs occuring, my precious marriage was in tatters from the unrelenting stress of householding through that epic chapter in time, I felt little inherent talent for parenting my beloved, spirited preschooler, and my husband wanted out. One day, lying lifeless on our bedroom floor, exhausted, drained, and depleted, a quiet voice inside me, from where I know not, whispered, "It's okay to let go." And, after a pause, I silently whispered back, "Okay, I give up, use me." At the time, the resignation felt both surprising and cliché. In hindsight, that was the moment when I had hit rock bottom, and, in the descending crash, the hard shell of my tenacious ego had been broken open, and my Soul was finally flooding out. As my ego shattered, my Soul had been set free to flow outside The Box. With no strength left, my weary, defeated, egoic will could no longer oppose the stronger force of Source. It was swept up and carried away with it. This moment was the turning point. The subsequent years of divorcing, returning to school, switching career tracks, and tenderly parenting an aching child while also grieving the end of life as I had believed it was supposed to be was a laborious feat. But I was on the beam, aligned with my truth, following my bliss. And it felt exhilarating.

"When the world seems to be falling apart," advised Joseph Campbell, "the rule is to hang onto your own bliss. It's that life that survives."[6] Getting off the beam, running off the rails, getting lost in the weeds is something we will be doing throughout our life until we learn the lesson of letting go of attachment—to outcome, to certainty, to The Picture, the accomplishments, the approval, the money, the stuff—and find our way back to The Path by following the crumbs of our bliss. This is the hero's and heroine's journey. "Keep breathing and moving toward the light," was my mantra. The light was whatever lit me up inside—my bliss. It made absolutely no sense to my fearful, limited mind. Thankfully, I had been sucked into The Flow of the powerful, omniscient, universal mind. Follow your bliss. Blossom into your fullest potential.

What is your heart's burning desire? What makes your pulse quicken and makes you excited to leap out of bed in the morning? That's your trailhead. Start there. And head in that direction. "Whatever makes you feel the sun from the inside out, chase that,"[7] wrote the Australian poet Gemma Troy. "When you recover or discover something that nourishes your soul and brings joy, care enough about yourself to make room for it in your life,"[8] encouraged Jean Shinoda Bolen, MD, and psychiatrist.

There may be plenty of noise in your head imploring you that this trailhead, this dream, is impractical, unrealistic, unsustainable, impossible, frightening, and a terrible mistake. Remember those guards—fear, doubt, and worry—at the edge of The Box? Their noise can stop you in your tracks, frozen in fear, and doubting your next step. They'll argue that what's best and safest for you is that your dream stays a daydream, and you run straight away back to the safe confines of The Box, as fast as possible. "We bury the faint crackling of our inner fire underneath other safer noises and settle for a false life,"[9] perceived David Brooks.

The safer noises in your head from those guards are extremely persuasive when trying to convince you of all the reasons why something won't work. There is no shortage of points it makes, and tales it tells. Acknowledge the wisdom of these guards, listen to their input, and act on it if necessary. Thank them for their noble attempt to protect you. And then ask them to now sit quietly in the back seat so you can hear and follow your heart and Soul. Honor the voices of fear, doubt, and worry when they show up, and simply never let them occupy the driver's seat. Ever.

"So many of us choose our path out of fear disguised as practicality," observed Jim Carrey. "What we really want seems impossibly out of reach and ridiculous to expect, so we never dare to ask the Universe for it. I'm the proof that you can ask the Universe for it. As far as I can tell, it's just about letting the Universe know what you want, and working toward it, while letting go of how it comes to pass. Your job is not to figure out how it's gonna happen for you, but to open the door in your head. And when the door opens in real life, just walk through it. Don't worry if you miss your cue, the Universe is constantly opening doors."[10] Keep the doors in your mind wide open.

Your limited mind cannot figure out the "how." Your job is to feel the "what." *What* is the desire burning in my heart? *What* is the call I hear? *What* is the pull I feel? *What* is my bliss? Your job is to trust that Source will guide you there. Source will take care of the how. Your job is to meet Source halfway by staying awake, and taking the steps, one by one, as the doors of opportunity open.

The story goes that the singer Billie Eilish had a heart's burning desire to be a "model" when she grew up. But she felt "chubby and short" and fell into a depression, believing she could never accomplish her dream. Perhaps the noise in her head, which had most likely been programmed there by everything she had ever seen in magazines and the media, said that she didn't look like a model—tall and thin. Apparently, she therefore retreated into her bedroom, sullen and depressed, and made music which came naturally to her. She inadvertently followed the pull to make music and stepped into The Flow. At some point, her brother Finneas invited her to collaborate. She walked through that door. Together, they wrote, sang and produced an album of songs which went on to win 10 Grammy awards that year, 2020. Billie became the second person, the youngest, and the first woman ever to sweep the "Big 4" categories at the music industry's pinnacle event. From there, she was catapulted into fame, and landed in designer clothing on the cover of fashion magazines. Becoming a model in her own right. And realizing her dream.

Her Path to becoming a model was convoluted. It wasn't a straight line, from Point A to Point B, as many of us mistakenly believe ours should be. We want to see our Path laid out clearly and smoothly in front of us before we take a step. We want to see a nice, safe path that doesn't awaken fear, doubt, and worry, and which ends with possessions and positions.

Billie Eilish eventually became a much greater type of model. One that her limited mind had no concept of. Simply by putting one foot in front of the other, surrendering to her music and doing what she loved, she inadvertently stepped onto the moving sidewalk. She had stepped into The Flow. And was led to a life far more interesting and fulfilling than her limited mind could ever have imagined, believed, or planned.

"If you're always trying to be normal you will never know how amazing you can be,"[11] remarked Maya Angelou, the phenomenally phenomenal American writer and civil rights activist who published numerous autobiographies, essays, books of poetry; has been credited with a list of plays, movies, and television shows spanning over 50 years; and received dozens of awards and honorary degrees. When we try to be normal, and follow The Map, we sacrifice our Soul, its longings, our Path, and our gift to the world—we inadvertently thwart the brilliance of Source's unbridled, mind-blowing expression.

Billie Eilish is no normal fashion model. She is an extraordinary fashion model. She is a Grammy-sweeping-singer-songwriter *Vogue* model. Plus, she is also a huge inspiration to millions of people who feel marginalized by what they see held up in the media as an ideal, acceptable, "perfect" model.

We miss out on our life if we sit on the sidelines and lament that it doesn't look the way we are taught and believe it should look, or is "supposed to" look. We miss our appointment with this moment— this one wild life—to work out in its own special way. Trust your

Path. "Where there is a way or path, it is someone else's path. You are not on your own path. If you follow someone else's way, you are not going to realize your potential,"[12] heeded Joseph Campbell.

Billie Eilish perhaps thought that "The Way" to become a model was "The Map to Becoming a Model." And, no doubt, The Only Map that "seasoned experts" in the industry see as The Way. Had she followed that well-worn map and taken the route laid out, she most likely would not have received acceptance as a model, and realized her fullest potential. And we would have all missed out on her true, innate brilliance and gifts. She forged her Path one step at a time, and becoming a fashion model wasn't the first, or only, step on her Path. "We must be willing to let go of the life we have planned so as to have the life that is waiting for us,"[13] advised Joseph Campbell.

Sometimes a step doesn't look appealing because we can't see where it will lead. We aren't absolutely certain it will lead us to where we think we want to go. So we won't take the step. Or, we take only those steps that we think, hope, and believe will get us to the destination our ego is seeking. "You cannot judge the beauty of a particular path just by looking at the gate,"[14] noticed Paulo Coelho.

Here's another fact for you: as Billie's story illustrates, generally there are several steps leading you to the step you desire. Trust that these other steps to get you there are either a shortcut or offer a needed, and helpful lesson. Continue to have the courage to follow your heart and intuition, even when the step looks out of place and nonsensical.

This was certainly true of my Path. At 50 years of age, and after several deeply fulfilling decades working happily as an art director in the glamorous and lucrative fashion advertising world,

including extensive travel to fascinating locations, and collabo-
rations with celebrities, my heart had a burning desire to study
massage therapy. "Wait, what?!!" said my ego. "NO. WAY."
And my head, with its limited programs, was having none of it,
"*Absolutely not!*" It didn't compute. It didn't fit The Picture. And
it didn't make financial sense. However, having crash landed
when hitting rock bottom, and being knocked senseless, I was
now in The Flow and found myself apprehensively signing up
to study. During the training, although my ego was trembling
with fear, doubt, and worry, my heart was jumping with joy and
clapping its hands, "Yes, this is bliss!" As I flowed through the
training, my heart felt a strong pull in the direction of teaching
yoga. "*Teach yoga?!*" My exasperated ego rolled its eyes, shook its
head, and let out a defeated sigh. At this point, my limited mind was
embracing the productive art of obliging my greater Soul, and
refrained from throwing up a stop sign or slamming on the breaks.
It simply said, "Okay. Let's." After walking through the door of
yoga training, a door to teaching opened, and I walked through.
Once on that step of the beam, an unexpected door marked
"meditation teacher" surprisingly and magically opened. And I
eagerly walked through. Eventually, I evolved and outgrew the
desire to be a professional massage therapist, and, like a snake
shedding its skin, left it behind to become a full-time yoga and
meditation teacher. As I taught, my happy heart longed to write a
book of collected wisdom teachings to help others. "Okay." said
my ego, "Let's!" As I was writing, the pandemic emerged, yoga
studios closed, and a colleague introduced me to the meaningful
work of life coaching. Helping others find their way felt fulfilling, and in alignment with my Center. I stayed on the beam and
went with The Flow. After studying and becoming a national board
certified life coach, a door to coaching opened, and I walked
through. I don't know what my heart will reach for next, but what
I do know is that I will eagerly follow its lead along my magical
mystery ride.

Joseph Campbell bequeathed, "Follow your bliss. If you do follow your bliss, you put yourself on a kind of track that has been there all the while waiting for you, and the life you ought to be living is the one you are living. When you can see that, you begin to meet people who are in the field of your bliss, and they open the doors to you. I say, follow your bliss and don't be afraid, and doors will open where you didn't know they were going to be. If you follow your bliss, doors will open for you that wouldn't have opened for anyone else."[15] When following your bliss, I can attest, the doors continue to open.

Following your bliss doesn't mean the trail will always be easy. You will encounter challenges as you follow your bliss. This is the nature of the exquisite human experience—challenges and gifts go together. But you will know you are on the right Path because of how you feel inside—you feel "right." You feel on track. You are on the beam. It's the inner riches, even with the challenges.

To flow outside The Box is to accept the hero's or heroine's journey. "The heroic life is living the individual adventure. There is no security in following the call to adventure. Nothing is exciting if you know what the outcome is going to be,"[16] continued Joseph Campbell. But here's the kicker: no one can know with certainty what the outcome is going to be because life is uncertain. So you may as well answer your call to adventure rather than huddle inside The Box. Of all the roads traveled, the individual adventure is the most satisfying. Stop calling it a daydream, start calling it your Path.

The writer and teacher Amara Honeck wrote, "To many of us, doing what makes our soul shine comes with some difficulty. There always seems to be something or someone standing in our way, or so we believe. My philosophy, and what has worked for me consistently, is to break goals down into small, attainable pieces. Otherwise, doing the things that make our soul shine can seem insurmountable. You must also overcome the idea that something or someone is standing in your way. There is always a positive way to go around an obstacle. Note: I did not say 'easy' but 'positive.' A way of moving around an obstacle that does not require taking away another's confidence or self-worth. You cannot make your soul shine by dimming the shine of another."[17]

Remember, the Path is a zigzag, not a straight line. There may be times when you feel lost. Maybe you've been marching to the beat of the "normal" drum for so long, aligned with the ego, that you have veered off course, run off the rails, or feel completely lost in the weeds. "It is so common for the greatest heroes to be separated from that which they know. It is an important factor to see that they've dealt with the loneliness that human beings experience,"[18] said John Bucher.

The writer Emily McDowell perceived, "'Finding yourself' is not really how it works. You aren't a ten-dollar bill in last winter's coat pocket. You are also not lost. Your true self is right there, buried under cultural conditioning, other people's opinions, and inaccurate conclusions you drew as a kid that became your beliefs about who you are. 'Finding yourself' is actually returning to yourself. An unlearning, an excavation, a remembering who you were before the world got its hands on you."[19]

Paulo Coelho looked at it this way: "Maybe the journey isn't so much about becoming someone. Maybe it's about getting rid of everything that isn't really you."[20] Excavate, and get rid of everything that isn't you—programs, beliefs, opinions. Including others' opinions. Everyone has an opinion. Many people believe that their opinion is gospel, and the only opinion that is right. And many people are more than happy to give you their well-intentioned yet unsolicited opinion. Parents are especially prone to this with their children. However, everyone else's opinion is colored by their past experience, beliefs, and mental programs. It's their experience, their story, not yours.

"No one is supposed to understand your calling. It wasn't a conference call," said some wise soul. What matters most is your opinion of yourself because no one knows you better than you. No one is living inside your skin, feeling the pull of your heart. "This life is mine alone," realized the author Glennon Doyle. "So I've stopped asking people for directions to places they've never been."[21] Continue to follow your own inner compass, moment by moment.

When we arrive at a particular place or achieve a specific goal, it's simply a moment in time, a step on our Path. It's not the point at which we sail smoothly into the sunset. Happily. Ever. After. The End. It's simply a milestone. A special bead on the strand. One of many. We continue to grow and evolve our whole life, until we take our last breath. When we embrace each moment, each step, with great love and great joy, the moments string together to create a life of great love and great joy.

Michelle Obama, the mom, attorney, and author, who served as the remarkably strong first African-American First Lady of the United States, when asked why she chose the word "becoming" for the title of her memoir, replied, "'Becoming' just summed it all up. In the preface, one of the things I say is ... a question that adults ask kids—that I hate, I think it's the worst question in the world—is, 'What do you want to be when you grow up?' As if growing up is finite, as if you become something and that is all there is. And my journey is the journey of always continually evolving. There is never a point where you arrive at a thing. And if you do, that's kind of sad, you know? If you think that there is a point in your life where you stop growing and you stop learning, that's sort of sad, because what else is left? I don't know what the next step will be...but the truth is, that for me, each decade has just uncovered something amazing that I would have never imagined. And if I had stopped looking, I would have missed out on so much. So I'm still becoming and I hope all of us know that we are constantly evolving."[22]

We are always in constant evolution, becoming one version of ourselves, and then learning and growing and evolving into a new version. "Life is a process of becoming," wrote Anaïs Nin, "a combination of states we have to go through. Where people fail is that they wish to elect a state and remain in it. This is a kind of death."[23] Clinging to a situation, or a moment, or The Fairytale Picture, or The Box, is a kind of death.

As we grow and evolve we must let go of what has come before in order to create what comes next. We must leave the step we are on and take the next step on our evolutionary journey. "As we choose, we step into a new reality forming in front of us of infinite possibility,"[24] realized the musician Trevor Oswalt. Each choice you make opens up a whole new, exciting world of possibilities and choices.

At one point in my early years, I heard that people, on average, change careers three times in their life. And I thought, "Not me! No way. I enjoy being a graphic design creative director and plan on doing it for the rest of my life." But then I outgrew my work. As I naturally evolved, I longed for something with deeper meaning, where I could help others. I began feeling discontent, inner poverty. The more I tried to hold onto a fixed destination, the more I suffered. Until the "fates dragged me," and—boom—a new career was born. Never say never. Although it was intensely challenging to feel my way along in the dark, switching tracks, it also felt intensely exhilarating and magical. It felt right. I woke up one day, years later, living with the deeper meaning that my heart had longed for—inspiring others. Not through graphic design art direction, but through teaching, coaching, writing, and speaking. I had to switch tracks. I let the Universe know *what* I wanted—deeper meaning and service—and worked toward it, while letting go of *how* it came to pass. I didn't figure out *how* it was going to happen. I simply felt the *what* in my heart, opened the doors in my mind, and walked through the doors of opportunity in my life as they opened onto a new track. My limited mind could absolutely not have dreamed up this mysterious and magical Path. I had to surrender to the omniscient, unlimited Source, and trust.

"First rule: Listen to your inner voice. Second rule: Be honest with yourself," explained Ram Dass. "The predicament is that you listen to your inner voice, and it leads you to a path, and then you outgrow it. And you don't want to admit that you've outgrown it, because you've made a big investment in it. But you must be willing to let go, to stand as naked as a newborn child, again and again, and again."[25] Shoshin. Beginner's mind. Always. That's how you Flow. Like a snake shedding a skin it's outgrown. Life, including your life, is a constant state of growth, shedding, and renewal. Summer, fall, winter, spring. Birth, life, death. The constant upward spiral of evolution. Allow it. Embrace it. Enjoy it.

Paula Kahumbu, Princeton University PhD, wildlife conservationist, and CEO of WildlifeDirect, said, "I became a filmmaker despite all the discouragement from others who reminded me that I am a trained ecologist.... None of us are limited by the skills we know. We have such extraordinary powers to explore and discover new talents, and our unique individual training becomes an asset, not our identity."[26] Our talents, training, and skills accumulate and transfer from step to step, building in collective strength.

Natalia Vodianova was born into poverty to a single mother in Gorky, Russia, helped care for her severely autistic younger sister, endured embarrassment and humiliation from peers, and sold fruit on the street in the black market to help her mother pay the bills. At the age of 17, she cut and refashioned one of her grandmother's skirts to create the miniskirt needed for a model "casting call" where a scout discovered her. On the plane ride from Russia to her first job in Paris, she recalled, the food on the plane was "by far" the best she'd ever eaten. She went on to become one of the most famous and celebrated fashion models of her time; a mother of five children; founder of the Naked Heart Foundation—a philanthropic organization committed to helping children with special needs and their families; a member of the Special Olympics International Board of Directors; and a United Nations Goodwill Ambassador. Her advice: "It's more about the journey, not about the goal because you never know really where you end up being. It's really about building the relationship with people you meet. Because this is what matters. It's what you take on with you in your next career, in the turn in your life."[27]

The powerhouse Eleanor Roosevelt, who was a mother of six; the longest-serving First Lady of the United States; a diplomat, and activist; a seven-year United States Delegate to the United Nations General Assembly; the first presidential spouse to hold regular press conferences, write a daily newspaper column, write a monthly magazine column, host a weekly radio show, and speak at a national party convention; and, by the time of her death, was regarded as "one of the most esteemed women in the world," stated, "The purpose of life, after all, is to live it, to taste the experience to the utmost, to reach out eagerly and without fear for newer and richer experience."[28]

There is no expiration date on new experiences, learning, growing, and evolving. You will be doing it until you take your last breath. An African proverb states, "When death finds you, may it find you alive!" Alive, meaning living it, tasting it, and continually reaching out eagerly for newer and richer experiences, walking your Path, not someone else's, not huddled inside The Box in quiet desperation, not clinging to a fixed destination or a picture, not limited by society's expectations, but still open to and participating in the constant process of personal evolution as long as you live. Sliding in sideways at the end, and yelling, "Whoa! What a ride!" That's alive!

"Your time is limited," bequeathed Steve Jobs, "so don't waste it living someone else's life. Don't be trapped by dogma, which is living with the results of other people's thinking. Don't let the noise of others' opinions drown out your own inner voice. And most important, have the courage to follow your heart and intuition. They somehow already know what you truly want to become. Everything else is secondary."[29]

20 | HEART

How do you navigate your way out of The Box and into The Flow? Have the courage to follow your heart. "A longing in your heart is holy. When your heart calls you, it's God...and you go,"[1] interpreted my friend Patricia Russo.

Carl Jung, the psychiatrist, psychoanalyst, and founder of analytical psychology, who is said to have believed that our main task in life is to discover and fulfill our deep, innate potential, advised, "Your vision will become clear only when you look into your heart."[2] Joseph Campbell, who spent his life studying and articulating The Hero's Journey, concurred, "Find what electrifies and enlivens your heart."[3] The wind of Source blows into the sail of your heart, and the rudder of your mind takes you there. The mind is used for the logistics of getting to where your heart is leading.

"You can't connect the dots looking forward," observed Steve Jobs, "you can only connect them looking backwards. So you have to trust that the dots will somehow connect in your future. You have to trust in something—your gut, destiny, life, karma, whatever. Because believing that the dots will connect down the road will give you the confidence to follow your heart even when it leads you off the well-worn path, and that will make all the difference."[4]

"Go confidently in the direction of your dreams. Live the life you've imagined,"[5] encouraged Henry David Thoreau, the 19-century, Harvard-educated writer and philosopher, who wrote the book *Walden,* which chronicled his own quest of following his heart by ventured away from the well-worn path of "respectable society" for a two year experiment, living a solitary, spiritual, and self-reliant life in a remote, and rudimentary cabin he built near a peaceful pond.

"Don't look for your dreams to come true, look to become true to your dreams,"[6] encouraged Michael Bernard Beckwith, minister. Your dreams don't just magically land in your lap, you must act on your dreams by consistently making choices in alignment with them. Your choices are the stepping stones to your dreams. Your choices bring your dreams to life. Trust The Path—the stepping stones—of your heart. "The future," said Eleanor Roosevelt, "belongs to those who believe in the beauty of their dreams."[7]

South African-born poet and author Iain Thomas wrote, "And every day, the world will drag you by the hand, yelling, 'This is important! And this is important! And this is important! You need to worry about this! And this! And this!' And each day, it's up to you to yank your hand back, put it on your heart and say, 'No. This is what's important.'"[8] Know your heart. Choose your heart. Act from your heart. "Your heart knows the way," wrote Rumi, "run in that direction."[9] And, "Wherever you go, go with all your heart,"[10] advised Confucius, the Chinese philosopher born over 2,500 years ago.

In a conversation with Arianna Huffington, Oprah Winfrey shared, "So many people ... have seen themselves in that whirlwind of living your life based on what other people wanted in the first place. And then you realize, 'But, is that really what *I* want? Why am I striving, striving, striving for that when what

I *really* feel, or what I *really* want...' It's like what we're talking about—being open to what your heart really desires and not being defined by what everybody else wants. The clarity of that." Ariannna agreed, "Yes, are we living *our* dream? Or are we living somebody else's dream or what society considers valuable, or what we watched in a movie? People have so many ideas about what success is that are not their ideas."[11]

"Do what you feel in your heart to be right, for you'll be criticized anyway,"[12] encouraged Eleanor Roosevelt. To feel what is right in your heart might sound quite simple yet it can be extremely challenging because of the fact that most of us have been conditioned away from following our heart. We are conditioned to follow our head, to the point where we lose all connection to our heart's wisdom and guidance.

We have been programmed to believe that our mind's ability to store, retrieve, and articulate facts—especially of the mathematical and scientific nature—is superior to all other abilities, and the only valuable ability worth developing. We, therefore, judge ourselves and each other based on the functioning of a small portion of the brain, to the exclusion of all else. And by doing so, we narrow our options in life to a suffocating and painful sliver. We each have vast talents in many different areas—linguistic, artistic, athletic, and empathetic, entrepreneurial, social, musical, and more. These talents are our gifts to the world. If we abandon them to align with the mind, or the ego, or The Map, or approval from others, we forfeit our reason for being here, we deny others the gift of our talents, and we deny Source's brilliant, uninhibited expression.

Our gift to the world, our reason for being here, lies in our heart, not our mind. "When you are born, your work is placed in your heart,"[13] wrote Khalil Gibran. Using your mind to navigate your

Path is like putting the cart before the horse and wondering why you aren't getting to the land of fulfillment. The poor mind. We ask too much of it. It is a wonderful servant, but a terrible master. Your mind serves your heart. Put the horse before the cart, choose to follow your heart.

"I looked in temples, churches, and mosques. But I found the Divine with my heart,"[14] realized Rumi. To revive the connection with your heart, spend time developing a relationship with it. The same way you develop a relationship with another person—spending time together, tuning in, asking questions, listening for answers, and responding for greater and greater intimacy and harmony. (See HEART FOCUS Meditation, page 93.)

To keep that channel of communication with the Divine wide open, clear your heart of darkness by noticing any resentments, grudges, bitterness, jealousy, revenge, contempt, hatred, and the like, which you may be harboring, and release those blocks. Work to keep this antenna for information from Source clear of debris.

According to the World Health Organization, in 2019, the number one cause of death on this whole globe was heart disease.[15] Disease, or dis-ease, is literally "not ease—the opposite of ease." As we examine our diet, exercise, sleep, stress, and vices in relation to heart dis-ease, perhaps we also need to examine our relationship with our heart? If we nurtured that relationship, maybe it would become stronger, more vibrant, and full of life?

Think of a small child trying to get its mother's attention. At first, the child may call her name, then tap her arm, then tug on her sleeve, before collapsing into a full-blown melt-down. Perhaps we aren't giving our heart the attention it needs to be heard? Or we aren't responding to its needs? Perhaps if we renewed our relationship with our heart by listening and responding, our heart health would improve? Honor your heart by respecting its longings and allowing it to guide you.

"What a joy to travel the way of the heart,"[16] reported Rumi. Your heart is your best friend. It is always with you. It will never leave you. It knows what is best for you and gives you the best advice, better than anyone else can. It is your guide. It will lead you on your authentic Path. It will never lead you astray. "The heart has its reasons, which reason does not know,"[17] realized Blaise Pascal, the 17th-century French philosopher, who, as a child prodigy in mathematics, knew a thing or two about reason.

"It is only with the heart that one can see rightly,"[18] observed the acclaimed French writer and poet Antoine de Saint-Exupéry. "Almost everything—all external expectations, all pride, all fear of embarrassment or failure—these things just fall away in the face of death, leaving only what is truly important. Remembering that you are going to die is the best way I know to avoid the trap of thinking that you have something to lose. You are already naked. There is no reason not to follow your heart,"[19] advocated Steve Jobs.

"The mind creates the abyss, the heart crosses it,"[20] taught Sri Nisargadatta Maharaj, an Indian guru. Listen to your heart. Follow your heart. Serve your heart. That's The Path.

21 | COURAGE

The word courage comes from the Latin root cor, which means heart. In one of its earliest forms, the word courage meant "to speak one's mind by telling one's heart." The word itself was created to describe expressing the contents of your heart.

Many of us feel afraid to express the contents of our hearts, afraid to be our true Self and live our true life because of fear—fear of failure, fear of loss, fear of loss of control, fear of condemnation, fear of humiliation, fear of rejection, fear of annihilation, fear of you-name-it, which all basically boils down to fear of pain.

"To create one's own world takes courage,"[1] reported Georgia O'Keeffe. Maybe this is why many of us must "hit rock bottom" before taking a step on The Path of the heart. We cling so tightly to the known path, the "safe" path, The Map, that it takes our lives falling apart in some major way to lose everything, including The Map. Hitting rock bottom is a spectacular gift in its own right. It knocks you senseless, cracking open the hard shell of your ego, and allowing your Source to flood out. You're finally fully alive, freely following your heart.

"Life," noticed Anais Nin, "shrinks or expands in proportion to one's courage."[2] To have courage—to express our heart's full contents—and live an expansive life, we must be brave, which means ready to face and endure danger or pain. Sometimes the next step feels easy, and nonthreatening. Sometimes the next step feels overwhelming and terrifying. This is when we need bravery to look danger or pain in the eye. When we remember that we are made of and guided by Source, it is much easier to be unflinchingly brave. It has given us the pull, and is taking us by the hand to the next step.

Irene Gut Opdyke, a Polish nurse, who, at the tender young age of 20, went to extraordinary lengths, and risked her life to safely hide and save 12 German Jews during the holocaust, shared, "Courage is a whisper from above. When you listen with your heart, you will know what to do and how and when."[3]

Once you've identified the next step, moving forward can feel a little like letting go of one trapeze and reaching for the next, without a safety net. Courage doesn't mean you don't feel afraid at times. We all feel fear at times. It's one of the keys on our emotional keyboard, it's part of the package of being human. "Fear is a reaction, courage is a decision,"[4] realized Winston Churchill, who is well known for his resolute leadership as Prime Minister of Great Britain when standing up to Nazi Germany during WWII.

Courage means you choose to be guided by your heart. Bravery means that you won't allow fear to hijack you, debilitate you, or pull you out of Flow and off The Path of your heart. Thank your fear for alerting you to potential danger, honor its wisdom by taking action if needed, and invite it to sit comfortably in the back seat as your heart continues to lead. When following your heart and taking risks feels scary, remember this: if it turns out the way you wanted, you will be delighted, and if not, you'll win a valuable lesson in order to be wiser and stronger for your next step. It's a win/win. You cannot lose.

22 | TRUST

This is where the rubber meets the road. This is the big one, the jumping off point. We can align with our heart, find clarity, make a choice, intend to take a step, and muster the bravery to step forward, but ultimately we must let go of the step we're on in order to take the next step, and enter The Flow.

Socrates, the ancient Greek philosopher and founder of Western Philosophy, born some 2,500 years ago, said, "To move the world we must move ourselves."[1] And this no one can do for you. No one can move your world and take that step but you. To realize your greatest potential, you must step. Life doesn't happen to you. It happens with you. "Either you do it like it's a big weight on you, or you do it as part of the dance,"[2] taught Ram Dass. You can do it like it's agony or like it's adventure.

Stepping forward on the unknown Path can feel a little like a scene in the movie *Raiders of the Lost Ark* when Harrison Ford's character, Indiana Jones, needs to cross a deep and wide ravine which his limited mind deems, "Impossible. Nobody can jump this." As he hears a "call" to believe, he realizes that he's going to have to take "a leap of faith." His only option is to believe and *trust*. He puts a trembling hand over his racing heart, and slowly, courageously, inches a foot forward. As he begins to lean forward, with agonizing trepidation, toward the yawning ravine,

121

a firm footbridge instantly and magically appears to support him across.[3] "Follow your bliss. And when you do, doors will open where you did not even know doors existed." The bridge will rise up. The step will appear.

Life is a mysterious unfolding in front of us. No one knows with certainty the experience of the next step until there. We need to take a leap of faith. This can feel scary—very, very scary. The noise in your head may increase its volume to capture your attention and try to lure you back into the protective shell of The Box. The doubt, the worry, the fear may surge. You may want to retreat into the familiar safety of your comfort zone. However, if you cling to the step you are on and resist moving forward into the pull, you will stagnate. Energy is meant to flow. Therefore trying to keep energy stagnant takes tremendous effort and is ultimately exhausting and depleting of your energy. "Living never wore one out so much as the effort not to live,"[4] deduced Anaïs Nin.

"It's a terrible thing, I think, in life to wait until you are ready," shared the prolific and accomplished English actor, author, comedian, director, musician and singer Hugh Laurie. "I have this feeling now that actually no one is ever ready to do anything. There is almost no such thing as ready. There is only now. And you may as well do it now. Generally speaking, now is as good a time as any."[5]

Know this: that the instinct to cling to the safety of The Box, or the current step, can definitely be part of the process of moving forward. The ability to move forward to the next step, and proceed with bravery, against the urge to retreat, requires only that you trust the greater power which gives you the desire, and guides you there—Source. This is so important, it bears repeating: the ability to move forward on your authentic Path and proceed with courage, against the urge to retreat, requires only that you trust the greater power which gives you both the dream, and the compass which guides you there.

You are Source manifested as a human being. And your longings are Source reaching for what it desires to create, and longs to express. Allow it. Surrender to it. Flow with it. Trust the power breathing you, and giving you life. Feed your trust, not your fear. Fear lessens when living on the wings of trust. As you move out onto the unknown next step of your Path, remember, you can only win. You will either win or win a lesson. Either way, you are choosing the exhilarating individual Path of the heart, which in itself is a wonderful gift, a win.

Maria Sharapova, the retired Russian professional tennis player and Olympic silver medalist, who was ranked number one in singles by the World Tennis Association on five separate occasions, and who was one of only ten women in the world, and the only Russian, to hold a career Grand Slam, encouraged, "I want anyone who dreams of excelling in anything to know that doubt and judgment are inevitable. Trust yourself. I promise you will prevail."[6]

Trust yourself. Ultimately, trust cannot be placed in anyone or anything outside yourself because all things are tenuous, not stable. All things have a birth, life, and death cycle that you cannot control. Yet, what lies behind you and what lies before you are tiny matters compared to what lies within you. "Fearlessness is like a muscle," said Arianna Huffington. "I know from my own life that the more I exercise it the more natural it becomes to not let my fears run me."[7]

The first step is usually the hardest to take. But once taken, you've set the wheels in motion. William H. Murray, the Scottish mountaineer who was part of the first expedition to ever reach the peak of the highest mountain in the world—Mount Everest—learned, "Until one is committed, there is hesitancy, the chance to draw back, always ineffectiveness. Concerning all acts of initiative (and creation), there is one elementary truth, the ignorance of which kills countless ideas and splendid plans: that the moment one definitely commits oneself, then Providence moves too. All sorts of things occur to help one that would never otherwise have occurred. A whole stream of events issues from the decision, raising in one's favour all manner of unforeseen incidents and meetings and material assistance, which no man could have dreamt would have come his way. I learned a deep respect for one of Goethe's couplets: 'Whatever you can do or dream you can, begin it. Boldness has genius, power and magic in it!'"[8]

"Begin to weave," encourages an old proverb, "and the divine will provide the thread." The doors begin to open. The bridges rise up to meet you. The support appears.

If stepping forward or jumping off feels terrifying, breathe. Train yourself to focus on your breathing, and gratitude. Breathing and gratitude. Keep putting one foot in front of the other where your heart leads, in the moment. Step onto the moving sidewalk. You can move in baby steps. One step at a time gets you up the mountain. Each day take one manageable step in the direction of your dream: make a phone call, google a fact, brainstorm with a friend.

Trust is defined as confident reliance on something when you are in a position of vulnerability. When you feel vulnerable, rely confidently on the Source which breathes life into you and breathes the dream into your heart. Trust is the turning point. Trust that you are part of something much bigger than your humanness. Your dreams are a piece of The One puzzle. Trust that if you fall, you will find treasure there—a lesson, wisdom—to strengthen you going forward. Trust that no matter what happens, the point of living is to enjoy the exhilaration of being alive, in this moment, at this time, on this earth.

"Whatever you're meant to do, do it now. The conditions are always impossible,"[9] advised Doris Lessing, the fiery and independent, British-Zimbabwean writer, who after leaving school at age 13, was self-educated, forged a colorful and unconventional life, and, at 88 years of age, was the oldest person ever to receive the Nobel Prize in Literature.

Interpreting the renowned economist Albert Hirschmann, the writer Jeff Haden said, "It's impossible to know how things will work out. So don't worry. While you can't know how things will turn out, what you can know is that doing something meaningful and fun will in itself be worth the effort. What you can know is that the process of pursuing whatever it is you want to pursue— if it's a goal you choose, desire, and believe in—is worth it, no matter what the result. You can't know the future. Don't try. Bet on yourself. Do what you think makes sense today."[10]

"Don't ever attach yourself to a person, a place, a company, an organization, or a project. Attach yourself to a mission, a calling, a purpose only. That's how you keep your power and your peace,"[11] offered the coach and author Adam Jablin.

What the unlimited Source has in store for you is always so much more infinitely wonderful than anything your limited mind can think up. Dream and then TRUST. Surrender to your heart's pull. Enjoy embodying the Universe in action.

23 | SERVE

You are unique. There is only one you. Therefore, just like your fingerprint, your talents are unique. You have something that no one else has exactly, and you are meant to contribute that for the benefit of all others. No one is superior to or inferior to another. We are all here with an equally special gift to share, to complement the whole, and help this world function like a well-oiled machine.

Use your gifts to serve others. And be cognizant of all those who offer their gifts in service to you—the people who grow your food and harvest it and cook it, bake it, package it, and ship it; the people who build the stores and hire the workers who stock the shelves and ring you up; the people who design your home and clothes and office; the builders, the decorators, and makers of chairs and beds, and paint; the plumbers and electricians and welders and carpenters; the people who entertain you—they sing, they dance, they act, they play sports; the coaches and teachers; the artists, the writers of songs and books and poems and scripts; those who make the microphones, cameras, computers, and technology; those who build the bridges and design the cars, planes, trains, and satellites, and put them all together; the sanitation and house-keeping workers; the healers and veterinarians; those working on renewable energy and sustainable systems for keeping this all going, etc. How often do you stop to contemplate, and give thanks to all your fellow human beings who spend their life energy sharing their gifts with you to make your world amazing?

"The ultimate aim of the quest must be neither release nor ecstasy for oneself, but the wisdom and the power to serve others,"[1] found Joseph Campbell.

Your every action is serving something. Before each action, ask, "What am I serving? Am I serving the call of my heart? Am I serving the call of my ego? Am I serving the well-being of my Self, and others? Am I serving the highest good of my Self, and others? Am I serving destruction? Construction? Love? Hate? Health? Illness? Am I serving acceptance? Compassion? Tolerance? Am I serving my neuroses? Or my gifts?"

When you are serving others with the gift of your talent, the whole world benefits. It's as though you are one piece in a 7 billion+ piece jigsaw puzzle. There is a hole in the great picture when you don't show up fully. Conversely, when you take up your piece in the puzzle, the whole picture is complete. Blossom into your place. We all need you there.

What is your gift? Think about what lights you up inside. What gets you leaping out of bed in the morning? What makes life worth living? That gift is the intersection of what you like, what you are good at, and how you can help the world—your "sweet spot." You were meant to be a contributing member of this world into which you were born.

"Don't ask what the world needs. Ask what makes you come alive and go do it. Because what the world needs is more people who have come alive,"[2] urged Howard Thurman, the African-American civil rights leader and theologian.

Enlightened leaders and luminaries throughout the ages have articulated the importance of individual actions in relation to the collective whole. In an assortment of essays and sermons, Martin Luther King, Jr., implored, "Life's most persistent and urgent question is, 'What are you doing for others?'"[3] President John F. Kennedy, in his inaugural address, inspired listeners to consider the virtues of service by saying, "Ask not what your country can do for you, ask what you can do for your country."[4] Audrey Hepburn, the actress and humanitarian, shared, "As you grow older, you will discover that you have two hands, one for helping yourself, and the other for helping others."[5]

We must ask ourselves what kind of world we wish to live in, and then create that. Be the change you wish to see. "How will you serve the world?" asked Jim Carrey. "What do they need that your talent will provide? That's all you have to figure out."[6]

24 | BREATH

As you walk to the edge of The Box to step or dive into The Flow, caution lights may flash—distracting you, scaring you, debilitating you. You can immediately find calm by anchoring your awareness into your breathing. We take our breath for granted. Most of us barely give it a moment's notice. Yet, the breath is a foundation. It's the first thing you do when you are born into this world, and the last thing you do before you pass on, and every moment in between. It never stops. It's always with you. It's a stable point to return to. Other aspects of your life come and go "like clouds in a windy sky." People, jobs, money, health, titles, relationship status, situations, you name it, will all come and go. All of life is impermanent. Coming together and falling apart. Yet, while you are alive, the breath is a constant.

When focused on the breath, you are no longer caught up in whatever wave of the moment is going up or down—be it a thought, emotion, sensation, or circumstance. It's as if you have climbed out of the waves and are resting on a raft. Your breath, then, is like a surfboard. Anchoring your focus onto your breath, as a surfer would a surfboard, allows you to ride the continuous ups and downs of your life with stability, equanimity, calm, and joy!

In his TEDx talk "Breathe to Heal," Max Strom, speaker, teacher and author, shared a study on breathing done at Stanford Research Institute, where "they took combat veterans with post-traumatic stress syndrome from Iran and Iraq, and taught them yoga and breathing. The facilitator, Emma Seppälä, PhD, a Stanford scholar said, 'It was mostly the breathing that affected them. We had them do this program for 3 months, and their PTSD symptoms were gone. And they didn't return, even a year later.' The US Defense Department is now advocating breathing and yoga for veterans. The Defense Department! Navy SEALs use breathwork to help them focus and calm before they go into battle. Navy SEALs are not new age, cuddly people. Navy SEALs only use technologies that work. They will not use anything else. Benefits of intentional breathwork are focus, calm, non-reactiveness, which we could all use."[1]

Whether you are a Navy SEAL going into action, or someone putting the next foot forward on your Path, the breath is your anchor. Conscious breathwork turns the fight or flight switch off, and the rest and digest switch on. "You can't calm the storm so stop trying. What you can do is calm yourself,"[2] clarified the writer Timber Hawkeye.

Dr. Andrew Weil, a Harvard-trained MD who helped establish the field of integrative medicine—an approach to wellness that combines conventional treatments like drugs, surgery, and lifestyle changes, with complementary therapies such as massage, meditation, and acupuncture, to treat the whole person in body, mind, and spirit—found, "Breathing is the most central, vital function of life.... Regulation of the breath can allow you to achieve mental equanimity. The most effective anti-anxiety measure that I know is simple regulation of breathing."[3] The breath is the foundation of your life. Without the breath, you do not have a human life. Strengthen your breathing in order to strengthen your life.

As you surrender to The Flow, and face any fear that may be triggered, the effort required is simply to keep breathing and moving toward the light. One step at a time creates your journey. One conscious breath at a time creates your journey with calm, balance, and joy.

BREATHING TECHNIQUES

These breathing techniques can be done any time and anywhere and repeated as often as necessary.

THE SQUARE BREATH
Exhale to empty your lungs completely.
On the next inhale, inhale for a count of 4,
hold for a count of 4, exhale for a count of 4,
and hold for a count of 4. Repeat 2 more times.
Return to your natural rhythm of breathing.

~

THE RESTORATION BREATH
The Restoration Breath is an ancient breathing technique
meant to rest and restore the nervous system.
Exhale to empty the lungs completely.
Inhale for a count of 4,
hold for a count of 7,
exhale for a count of 8.
Repeat 2 more times.
And return to your natural rhythm of breathing.

~

25 | REVERENCE

Reverence is defined as a feeling of profound respect and awe. Without reverence, life is flat, shallow, and meaningless. With reverence we experience the rapture of being alive. Lack of reverence is to skim the surface. Embodying reverence is to take the deepest dive into this rich, abundant life.

Instead of racing through your days from one activity to the next, skimming the surface, enjoy the deeper dive by appreciating whatever is happening in the present moment. "Wow, this is what a chirping bird sounds like, and this is the feeling of happiness which is triggered inside me as I hear it. Wow, this is what warmth in my heart feels like when I'm happy. Wow, this is what it feels like to watch the sunset on the ocean and the sky turn to colors of pink and orange and yellow. Wow, this is what it feels like to have expectations that are dashed. Wow, this is what it feels like to have the volcano of anger exploding inside of me. Wow, this is what it feels like to sit at the dining table and eat with my family. Wow, this is what it feels like to have a meaningful discussion with another human being." Etc, etc, etc.

Shift from "have to" to "get to." You get to feel. You get to experience a life as a human. You get to feel pleasure and pain. You get to feel anticipation and disappointment. You get to experience butterflies in your stomach or a lump in your throat or a broken heart. You get to receive blessings, and pearls of wisdom. You get to feel struggle and challenge. You get to wake up in the morning to a brand new, fresh day. You get to go to work. You get to experience conflict and harmony with family and colleagues. You get to pick up your kids or visit your parents or clean the house or make dinner. You get to hear thunder and lightning or ocean waves crashing or your loved one's voice or the wind in the trees or music that lifts your Soul. You get to taste delicious flavors, and smell delightful scents. You get to experience this whole smorgasbord of life on earth as a human. What a spectacular gift. It won't last forever—it's finite. Enjoy it while it lasts.

Pema Chödrön once described an article her teacher, Trungpa Rinpoche, had written regarding depression. "He described so vividly what depression felt like that you knew that he knew what it was like to be depressed. And he said, 'It's so juicy! It has so much energy in it. It's one of the best! It's really powerful. It's a wonderful one to contact directly.' It was clear that Rinpoche himself had worked with it that way."[1] His response to depression was, "Wow! This is what it's like to feel depressed as a human!" He shifted his whole perspective from being swallowed up by the feelings, drowning in them, and working to avoid them, to instead focusing on appreciating the wonder of having this experience—being a human, walking this earth, and feeling this particular emotion.

I have learned to use this perspective with all of my emotions. "Wow, this is what joy feels like! This is what pain feels like! This is what passion feels like! Contentment, suffering, elation, ecstasy. Anger and rage. Sadness. Jealousy. Frustration. Fear. Wow." I get to be alive and experience the whole smorgasbord of human feelings. For that I feel grateful. And this has made all the difference in the world. This has made my life an appreciated adventure rather than an agonizing ordeal.

The British meditation teacher Burgs put it this way: "It doesn't actually take very much to make the deepest part of us incredibly happy. Just to be here, just to … appreciate being here—to feel that you're alive, to be in touch with your heart. That's it. It takes mindfulness to come to a human life. The chance to be part of this happens briefly. The invitation is how much you can notice what you're already part of. And appreciate it and share it. And care about those that are around you, count for their welfare while you are looking out for your own. That's it. And then you'll get to the end of it, having had an awesome time, knowing … that is something you'd recommend to others. It's really simple. When you came here, you came here with a sense of awe and wonder, dying to just see what it's about. You know, it's like, 'What would it be like to be down there, to be part of it?' And you came here with a sense of wonder."[2]

Here you are. You're "down here." Seeing what it's all about. Some things are a joy to experience, some things are a pain to experience. But a shift in perspective from despair: "This is awful," to wonder: "Wow! This is what it feels like to experience 'x, y, or z' as a human," can immediately transform an ordeal into an adventure. Embodying reverence for each moment of this spectacular, wonder-full, human experience allows you to feel the rapture of being alive.

"Suddenly you're ripped into being alive. And life is pain, and life is suffering, and life is horror, but my god you're alive and it's spectacular,"[3] effused Joseph Campbell.

All of it, this whole human opera—the highs, the lows, the agony, the ecstasy—can be seen through the eyes of wonder and awe.

You are not only at the show with a ringside seat, you're an actor on the stage. You're part of the dance of the Universe. You *are* the Universe in action. Holy cow! You can appreciate whatever is happening in the present moment by simply shifting from your limited human perspective—skimming the surface, into your limitless Soul perspective—diving deeply into reverence for your life. "All I can say about life is, 'Oh, God, enjoy it!'"[4] offered Bob Newhart, the American actor and comedian.

This life is a gift. All of it. The whole enchilada. When things go your way, say thank you and celebrate. When things don't go your way, say thank you and celebrate the lesson. Joyfully navigate an authentic, exhilarating life full of deep inner fulfillment and savor this most awesome human adventure while you have it. Keep breathing and moving toward the light. Flow outside The Box.

~

NOTES

INTRODUCTION

1. Joseph Campbell, *Myths to Live By* (Viking, 1972).

2. Buddha, https://www.goodreads.com/quotes/181
5-Do-not-believe-in-anything-simply-because-you-have-heard.

1 | THE BOX

1. C.G. Jung, *Modern Man in Search of a Soul* (Kegan Paul, Trench,
Trubner and Co, London, 1933).

2. Anais Nin, *The Early Diary of Anais Nin Vol 4.* (Mariner Books, United
Kingdom, 1986).

2 | THE FLOW

1. Rumi, *The Essential Rumi*, https://www.goodreads.com/quotes/736
0487-Let-yourself-be-silently-drawn-by-the-stronger-pull-of.

2. Seneca, https://www.goodreads.com/quotes/409452-The-fates-lead-those
-who-will-those-who-won-t-they.

3. Joseph Campbell, https://quotefancy.com/quote/15906/
Joseph-Campbell-If-you-are-falling-dive.

4. Franz Kafka, https://www.goodreads.com/quotes/9958144-every-thing
-you-love-is-very-likely-to-be-lost.

5. Richard Branson, https://twitter.com/richardbranson/
status/682208324352393217?lang=en.

6. Vincent Van Gogh, https://quoteinvestigator.com/2016/06/18/passionate/.

7. Oprah Winfrey, Wellesley College Commencement speech, 1997;
https://www.youtube.com/watch?v=Bpd3raj8xww.

3 | THE MAP

1. Steve Jobs, Stanford Commencement speech, 2005;
https://www.youtube.com/watch?v=Hd_ptbiPoXM.

2. Joseph Campbell, https://www.goodreads.com/author/quotes/20105.
Joseph_Campbell.

4 | SOURCE

1. https://www.livescience.com/50881-first-law-thermodynamics.html.

2. Joseph Campbell, https://www.jcf.org/works/quote/
the-universal-doctrine-teaches/.

3. Thich Nhat Hanh, *Living Buddha, Living Christ 10th Anniversary
Edition* (Penguin, 2007), 138.

4. Carl Sagan, *Cosmos* (Random House, 1980).

5. Dr. Ashley King, https://www.nhm.ac.uk/discover/
are-we-really-made-of-stardust.html.

6. Rumi, https://www.goodreads.com/quotes/643821-i-searched
-for-god-and-found-only-myself-i-searched.

7. Max Planck, *The New Science* (Meridian Books, 1st edition, 1959).

8. Joseph Campbell, *An Open Life: Joseph Campbell in Conversation with Michael Toms* (Harper Perennial, 1990).

9. Alan Wilson Watts, https://www.youtube.com/watch?v=MITcdxtO374.

10. Oprah Winfrey, Wellesley College Commencement speech, 1997; https://www.youtube.com/watch?v=Bpd3raj8xww.

11. Thich Nhat Hanh, *Living Buddha, Living Christ 10th Anniversary Edition* (Penguin, 2007), 138.

12. Ram Dass, Facebook, Ram Dass, Love Serve Remember, February 16, 2012.

5 | EGO

1. Georgia O'Keeffe, Facebook, Georgia O'Keeffe Museum, July 27, 2019.

2. David Brooks, *The Second Mountain* (Random House, 2020).

6 | PERFECTION

1. Stephen Hawking, *Into the Universe*, Discovery Channel, 2010.

2. Karla McLaren, *The Language of Emotions* (Sounds True, Incorporated, 2010).

3. Anais Nin, *Henry and June: The Unexpurgated Diary of Anais Nin* (Harcourt Trade Publishers, 1986).

4. Pema Chödrön, *When Things Fall Apart: Heart Advice for Difficult Times* (Shambhala Publishing, 1996).

5. Anna Quindlen, Mount Holyoke Commencement speech, 1999; https://www.c-span.org/video/?123622-1/mount-holyoke-college-commencement-speech.

6. Joseph Campbell, *A Joseph Campbell Companion, Reflections on the Art of Living* (Harper Perennial, 1995).

7. Yoyo Ma, https://www.youtube.com/watch?v=dbjgHkj-syM.

7 | SUCCESS

1. Jim Carrey, Maharishi University of Management Commencement speech, 2014; https://www.youtube.com/watch?v=V80-gPkpH6M.

2. Joseph Campbell, *The Power of Myth* (Doubleday, 1988).

3. Seane Corn, Facebook, May 5, 2016.

4. Anna Quindlen, Mount Holyoke Commencement speech, 1999; https://www.c-span.org/video/?123622-1/mount-holyoke-college-commencement-speech.

5. Joseph Campbell, *A Joseph Campbell Companion, Reflections on the Art of Living* (Harper Perennial, 1995).

6. Richard Branson, https://etcanada.com/video/1548598851859/et-canada-connects-richard-branson/.

7. Warren Buffett, https://www.youtube.com/watch?v=6XFwlNVRD5M.

8. Steve Jobs, Stanford Commencement speech, 2005; https://www.youtube.com/watch?v=Hd_ptbiPoXM.

9. Oprah Winfrey, Stanford Commencement speech, 2008; https://www.youtube.com/watch?v=Bpd3raj8xww.

10. Ralph Waldo Emerson, https://www.goodreads.com/quotes/14785-Nothing-great-was-ever-achieved-without-enthusiasm.

11. Georgia O'Keeffe, Facebook, Georgia O'Keeffe Museum, June 14, 2021.

12. Thích Nhất Hạnh, https://www.goodreads.com/quotes/376441-at-any-moment-you-have-a-choice-that-either-leads

8 | FAILURE

1. Arianna Huffingtson, https://www.oprah.com/own-super-soul-sunday/full-episode-Oprah-and-arianna-huffington-on-her-big-wake-up-call.

2. Alyssa Satara, https://www.inc.com/alyssa-sataraarianna-huffington-said-this1-thing-showed-us-how-to-get-closer-to-success.html.

3. Paulo Coelho, *The Alchemist* (HarperTorch, 1988).

4. Richard Bach, https://www.azquotes.com/quote/676992.

5. Oprah Winfrey, Stanford Commencement speech, 2008; https://www.youtube.com/watch?v=Bpd3raj8xww.

6. Thomas Edison, https://quoteinvestigator.com/2012/07/31/edison-lot-results/.

7. Sonia Sotomayor, https://www.huffpost.com/entry/sonia-sotomayor-rhode-island-commencement speech_n_57422f1fe4b0613b512a9335.

8. Oprah Winfrey, Wellesley College Commencement speech, 1997; https://www.youtube.com/watch?v=Bpd3raj8xww.

9. JK Rowling; Harvard University commencement speech, 2008; https://www.youtube.com/watch?v=wHGqp8lz36c.

10. Miles Davis, https://www.saxontheweb.net/threads/nicholas-payton-on-why-jazz-isnt-cool-anymore.385472/.

11. Joseph Campbell, *A Joseph Campbell Companion, Reflections on the Art of Living* (Harper Perennial, 1995), 24.

12. Carl Jung, https://www.goodreads.com/quotes/50795-i-am-not-what-happened-to-me-i-am-what.

13. Nelson Mandela, https://www.goodreads.com/quotes/270163-Do-not-judge-me-by-my-successes-judge-me-by.

9 | CHALLENGE

1. Anne Bradstreet, https://www.goodreads.com/quotes/136895-if-we-had-no-winter-the-spring-would-not-be.

2. Dolly Parton, https://twitter.com/dollyparton/status/1242587160525647872?lang=en.

3. Martin Luther King, Jr., "I've Been to the Mountaintop," delivered April 3, 1968, Mason Temple (Church of God in Christ Headquarters, Memphis, Tennessee).

4. Thich Nhat Hanh, https://plumvillage.org/about/thich-nhat-hanh/ interviews-with-thich-nhat-hanh/san-francisco-chronicle-sunday-interview-october-12-1997/#filter=.topics-buddhism.

5. Bernice Johnson Reagan, https://www.goodreads.com/quotes/51340-Life-s-challenges-are-not-supposed-to-paralyze-you-they-re-supposed.

6. Joseph Campbell, https://quotefancy.com/quote/61417/Joseph-Campbell-Opportunities-to-find-deeper-powers-within-ourselves-come-when-life-seems.

7. JK Rowling, Harvard University Commencement speech, 2008; https://www.youtube.com/watch?v=wHGqp8lz36c.

8. Lao Tzu, *Tao Te Ching*; https://www.goodreads.com/quotes/1210012-if -you-want-to-become-whole-let-yourself-be-partial#:~:text=If%20you%20 want%20to%20become%20straight%2C%20let%20yourself%20be%20cr-ooked,given%20everything%2C%20give%20everything%20up.

9. Paulo Coelho, *Eleven Minutes* (Rocco, 2003).

10. John Bucher, https://www.jcf.org/why-we-rise/.

11. Khalil Gibran, https://www.goodreads.com/quotes/3899-Out-of-suffering-have-emerged-the-strongest-souls-the-most.

14. Nelson Mandela, https://www.inc.com/jim-schleckser nelson-mandela-s-secret-to-winning.html.

15. Kabir, http://www.quoterumi.com/category/kabir/.

10 | PAIN

1. Joseph Campbell, *The Power of Myth with Bill Moyers* (Doubleday, 1988), 66.

2. Joseph Campbell, https://www.goodreads.com/quotes/373467-find-a-place-inside-where-there-s-joy-and-the-joy.

3. Vivienne Greene, https://www.goodreads.com/author/quotes/769264. Vivian_Greene.

4. Jon Kabat Zinn, https://www.goodreads.com/quotes/331826-you-can-t-stop-the-waves-but-you-can-learn-to.

5. Robert Kyosaki, *Rich Dad Poor Dad* (Warner Books, 2000).

6. Steve Maraboli, https://www.goodreads.com/quotes/319000-life-doesn-t-get-easier-or-more-forgiving-we-get-stronger.

11 | PERSEVERANCE

1. Albert Camus, https://www.goodreads.com/quotes/1182701-Sometimes-carrying-on-just-carrying-on-is-the-superhuman-achievement.

2. https://www.huffingtonpost.co.uk/entry ages-famous-people-got-big-break-Facebook-status_uk_5721f18ee4b0a1e971cb20f6.

3. Steve Jobs, Stanford Commencement speech, 2005; https://www.youtube.com/watch?v=Hd_ptbiPoXM.

4. Lao Tzu, https://www.goodreads.com/quotes/21535-the-journey-of-a-thousand-miles-begins-with-a-single.

5. Martin Luther King Jr., *Let Nobody Turn Us Around: Voices on Resistance, Reform, and Renewal an African American Anthology* (Lanham, Rowman & Littlefield, 2000).

6. Brené Brown, Marie TV, "How to 'Brave the Wilderness' & Find True Belonging," 2017.

7. Diana Nyad, https://www.theartof.com/speakers/diana-nyad.

8. Diana Nyad, https://www.cbsnews.com/news/diana-nyad-on-epic-swim-my-mantra-was-find-a-way/.

9. Ralph Waldo Emerson, https://www.goodreads.com/quotes/15579-What-lies-behind-us-and-what-lies-before-us-are.

10. Diana Nyad, *The Wisdom of Sundays* (Flatiron Books, New York, 2017), 182.

11. https://www.augustachronicle.com/story/opinion/ editorials/2015/12/13/ find-your-way/14344212007/.

12 | THE MIND

1. Brené Brown, *Rising Strong* (Random House Publishing Group, 2015).

2. https://www.ncbi.nlm.nih.gov/pmc/articles/PMC3652533/.

3. David James Lee, https://soundcloud.com/wu-wei-wisdom/ be-mindful-of-your-self-talk-its-A-conversation-with-the-universe.

4. Dr.Vernon Williams, https://www.thehealthy.com/mental-health/ mindfulness-quotes/.

5. Alvin Toffler, *Future Shock* (Random House, 1970).

6. Shunryu Suzuki, https://buddhamind.works/shunryu-suzuki/.

7. Georgia O'Keeffe, Facebook, Georgia O'Keeffe Museum, March 22, 2021.

8. Richard Branson, https://www.virgin.com/branson-family/ richard-branson-blog/8-tips-living-your-best-life.

9. Steve Jobs, Stanford Commencement speech, 2005; https://www.youtube.com/watch?v=Hd_ptbiPoXM.

10. Pablo Picasso, https://www.goodreads.com/quotes/62706- It-took-me-four-years-to-paint-like-raphael-but.

11. James Allen, *As a Man Thinketh* (Simon & Schuster, 1903).

12. Thich Nhat Hanh, *Anger* (Penguin., 2001), 75.

13. Marie Forleo, https://www.facebook.com/ watch/?v=10155537912803978.

14. Marcus Aurelius, https://www.goodreads.com/author/quotes/17212 Marcus_Aurelius.

15. Helen Gurley Brown, *Wise Women* (Bulfinch Press, 2002), 46.

16. Thich Nhat Hanh, *Teachings on Love* (Parallax Press, 1995).

17. Gay Hendricks, *The Big Leap* (HarperCollins, 2009).

18. Brené Brown, "Summer Sister Series on The Gifts of Imperfection, Part 3 of 6," July 7, 2021.

19. Laura Wilkinson, https://www.youtube.com/watch?v=BYR52_F8bug.

20. Laura Wilkinson, https://www.laurawilkinson.com/about.

21. Oprah Winfrey, Wellesley College Commencement speech, 1997; https://www.youtube.com/watch?v=Bpd3raj8xww.

13 | EMOTIONS

1. Thích Nhất Hạnh, *Stepping into Freedom: Rules of Monastic Practice for Novices* (Parallax Press, 1997).

2. Pema Chodron, https://tricycle.org/magazine/meditating-emotions/.

3. Susan David, PhD, https://twitter.com/susandavid_phd/status/1118273908078104576?lang=en.

4. India Arie, *The Wisdom of Sundays* (Flatiron Books, New York, 2017), 183.

5. Georgia O'Keeffe, https://www.goodreads.com/quotes/59275-i-ve-been-absolutely-terrified-Every-moment-of-my-life-and.

6. Amanda Gorman, https://www.nytimes.com/2022/01/20/opinion/amanda-gorman-poem-inauguration.html?smid=fb-share&fbclid=IwAR0BoDHvLPwSoaGeL75LHa7y8ndc1opzS1eMp_2De6AAd7VQhAeJXDdJpCU

7. Susan David, PhD, https://www.ted.com/talks/susan_david_the_gift_and_power_of_emotional_courage/transcript?language=en.

8. Thích Nhất Hạnh, *Old Path White Clouds: The Life Story of the Buddha* (Parallax Press, 1987).

14 | THE BODY

1. Oprah Winfrey, Stanford Commencement speech, 2008; https://www.youtube.com/watch?v=Bpd3raj8xww.

2. Martha Graham, *Blood memory* (Doubleday, 1991).

16 | INTUITION

1. Steve Jobs, Stanford Commencement speech, 2005; https://www.youtube.com/watch?v=Hd_ptbiPoXM.

2. Rumi, https://www.goodreads.com/quotes/7440878-there-is-a-voice-that-doesn-t-use-words-listen.

3. Oprah Winfrey, Wellesley College Commencement speech, 1997; https://www.youtube.com/watch?v=Bpd3raj8xww.

4. Barbara Walters, Yale Commencement speech, 2012.

5. Mary Morrissey, Source unknown.

6. Steve Jobs, Stanford Commencement speech, 2005; https://www.youtube.com/watch?v=Hd_ptbiPoXM.

7. Ram Dass, babaramdass instagram post, November 13, 2021.

8. Oprah Winfrey, oprahdaily instagram post, January 13, 2022.

17 | QUIET

1. Ram Dass, *Be Here Now* (Lama Foundation, San Cristobal, New Mexico, 1971).

2. Lupita Nyong'o, https://www.ellevatenetwork.com/articles/7922-quotes-about-following-your-dreams.

3. Joseph Campbell, https://www.goodreads.com/author/quotes/20105. Joseph_Campbell?page=2.

4. Shunryu Suzuki Roshi, https://leifurl.blog.is/blog/leifurl/entry/1717834/.

5. Thích Nhất Hạnh, *The Power of Quiet in a World Full of Noise* (HarperOne, 2015).

18 | MEDITATION

1. Oprah Winfrey and Arianna Huffington, "Super Soul Sunday," Season 5 Episode 511, 5/11/2014.

2. Thich Nhat Hanh, *The Miracle of Mindfulness: An Introduction to the Practice of Meditation* (Beacon Press, 1975).

3. Joseph Campbell, *A Joseph Campbell Companion: Reflections of the Art of Living* (Harper Perennial, 1995).

4. Steve Jobs, *Steve Jobs: A Biography by Walter Isaacson* (Simon & Schuster, 2011).

5. Thomas Edison, https://www.linkedin.com/pulse/morning-coffee-your-weekly-Fill-up-mind-spirit-strike-sandra-nickel.

6. Oprah Winfrey, oprah.com; "What Oprah Knows About the Power of Meditation"; https://www.oprah.com/inspiration/what-oprah-knows-about-the-power-of-meditation.

7. youtube.com/watch?v=NJ9UtuWfs3U

8. Joseph Campbell, *A Joseph Campbell Companion, Reflections on the Art of Living* (Harper Perennial, 1995), 208.

9. Paramahansa Yogananda, https://quotefancy.com/quote/884702/Paramahansa-Yogananda-The-soul-loves-to-meditate-for-in-contact-with-the-Spirit-lies-its.

19 | THE PATH

1.Henry David Thoreau, *Walden* (Ticknor and Fields: Boston, 1854).

2. Hunter S. Thompson, *The Proud Highway: Saga of a Desperate Southern Gentleman, 1955-1967* (Ballantine Books, 1997).

3. Joseph Campbell, https://www.jcf.org/works/quote/the-big-question/.

4. Thich Nhat Hanh, https://www.goodreads.com/quotes/376441-At-any-moment-you-have-a-choice-that-either-leads.

5. Joseph Campbell, *The Power of Myth* (Doubleday, 1988), 229.

6. Joseph Campbell, *A Joseph Campbell Companion, Reflections on the Art of Living* (Harper Perennial, 1995).

7. Gemma Troy, Facebook, Gemma Troy Poetry, April 15, 2020.

8. Jean Shinoda Bolen, MD, https://www.shinebright.us/post/make-room-for-joy.

9. David Brooks, *The Second Mountain* (Random House, 2020).

10. Jim Carrey, Maharishi University of Management Commencement speech, 2014; https://www.youtube.com/watch?v=V80-gPkpH6M.

11. Maya Angelou, https://www.bbc.com/news/world-us-canada-27610770.

12. Joseph Campbell, *Pathways to Bliss* (New World Library, 2004).

13. Joseph Campbell, *A Joseph Campbell Companion: Reflections on the Art of Living* (Harper Perennial, 1995).

14. Paulo Coelho, *Warrior of the Light* (HarperCollins, 2021).

15. Joseph Campbell, *A Joseph Campbell Companion: Reflections on the Art of Living* (Harper Perennial, 1995).

16. Joseph Campbell, https://www.facebook.com/josephcampbellcompanion/posts/follow-your-bliss-the-heroic-life-is-living-the-individual-adventure-there-is-no/1154874601277142/

17. Amara Honeck, https://www.amarahoneck.com/post/do-what-makes-your-soul-shine.

18. John Bucher, Source unknown.

19. Emily McDowell, Excerpt from "Finding Yourself" Card + Journal | Available at emilymcdowell.com © Knock Knock LLC.

20. Paulo Coelho, https://twitter.com/paulocoelho/status/1010864837784690689?lang=en.

21. Glennon Doyle, https://www.instagram.com/p/CDhuT3Vhc4W/.

22. Michelle Obama, https://www.youtube.com/watch?v=FfN5O0I_DVE.

23. Anais Nin, *D.H. Lawrence: An Unprofessional Study* (Swallow/OUP, 1964).

24. Trevor Oswalt, "Can't Fall Out Of Love," East Forest.

25. Ram Dass, Facebook, Ram Dass Love Serve Remember, January 23, 2021.

26. Paula Kahumbu, Personal correspondence.

27. Natalia Vodianova, YouTube, "How I Got Discovered" with Derek Blasberg, January 24, 2020.

28. Elenor Roosevelt, *You Learn by Living: Eleven Keys for a More Fulfilling Life* (Harper Perennial, 2016).

29. Steve Jobs, Stanford Commencement speech, 2005; https://www.youtube.com/watch?v=Hd_ptbiPoXM.

20 | HEART

1. Patricia Russo, Facebook, July 2021.

2. Carl Jung, https://www.reddit.com/r/Jung/comments/1bptva/in_what_essay_did_carl_jung_say_your_vision_will/.

3. Joseph Campbell, *The Hero's Journey* (HarperCollins, 1990).

4. Steve Jobs, Stanford Commencement speech, 2005; https://www.youtube.com/watch?v=Hd_ptbiPoXM.

5. Henry David Thoreau, *Walden*; https://en.wikiquote.org/wiki/Talk:Henry_David_Thoreau.

6. Michael Beckwith, Facebook, Michael Bernard Beckwith, September 19, 2015.

7. Elenor Roosevelt, https://quoteinvestigator.com/2018/02/10/beauty-dreams/.

8. Iain Thomas, *I wrote this for you 2007-2017* (Central Avenue Publishing, 2017).

9. Rumi, https://www.goodreads.com/quotes/9941552-Your-heart-knows-the-way-run-in-that-direction.

10. Confucious, https://www.goodreads.com/quotes/8496573-wherever-you-go-go-with-all-your-heart.

11. Oprah Winfrey and Arianna Huffington, "Super Soul Sunday," Season 5 Episode 511, May 11, 2014.

12. Eleanor Roosevelt, https://www.goodreads.com/quotes/7737-Do-what-you-feel-in-your-heart-to-be-right.

13. Kahlil Gibran, https://www.azquotes.com/quote/1430662.

14. Rumi, https://www.goodreads.com/quotes/1063266-i-looked-in-temples-churches-and-mosques-but-i-found.

15. World Health Organization, https://www.who.int/news-room/fact-sheets/detail/the-top-10-causes-of-death.

16. Rumi, https://www.azquotes.com/quote/662949.

17. Blaise Pascal, *Pensées* (17th-century).

18. Antoine de Saint-Exupéry, *The Little Prince* (Reynal & Hitchcock, 1943).

19. Steve Jobs, Stanford Commencement speech, 2005; https://www.youtube.com/watch?v=Hd_ptbiPoXM.

20. Maharaj, https://www.goodreads.com/quotes/972631-the-mind-creates-the-abyss-the-heart-crosses-it.

21 | COURAGE

1. Georgia O'Keeffe, Facebook, Georgia O'Keeffe Museum, August 30, 2021.

2. Anais Nin, https://cartereducation.medium.com/quotes-in-context-anais-nin-life-shrinks-or-expands-according-to-ones-courage-9a6c160fc2c7

3. Irene Gut Opdyke, nbcnews.com, https://www.nbcnews.com/investigations/hero-holocaust-polish-housekeeper-saved-12-jews-rcna12833?utm_source=facebook&utm_medium=news_tab, January 27, 2022.

4. Winston Churchhill, https://www.goodreads.com/quotes/721301-Fear-is-a-reaction-courage-is-a-decision.

22 | TRUST

1. Socrates, https://www.goodreads.com/quotes/310475-To-move-the-world-we-must-move-ourselves.

2. Ram Dass, https://www.ramdass.org/shivas-dance-of-life/.

3. Indiana Jones, https://www.youtube.com/watch?v=q-JIfjNnnMA.

4. Anais Nin, *Anais Nin Reader* (Swallow/OUP, 1973), 111.

5. Hugh Laurie, https://www.goodreads.com/quotes/675179-It-s-a-terrible-thing-i-think-in-life-to-wait.

6. Maria Sharapova, https://www.vanityfair.com/style/2020/02/Maria-sharapova-steps-away-from-the-game.

7. Arianna Huffington, https://www.entrepreneur.com/article/279062.

8. William H. Murray, *The Scottish Himalayan Expedition* (Dent, London, 1951).

9. Doris Lessing, Attributed; source unknown.

10. Jeff Haden, https://www.inc.com/jeff-haden/malcolm-gladwell-says-3-words-separate-people-Who-achieve-from-those-who-only-daydream.html.

11. Adam Jablin, https://adamjablin.com/.

23 | SERVE

1. Joseph Campbell, *The Power of Myth* (Doubleday, 1988).

2. Howard Thurman, https://www.azquotes.com/quote/518260.

3. Martin Luther King, Jr., https://quoteinvestigator.com/2016/01/18/altruism/.

4. John F. Kennedy, https://www.jfklibrary.org/learn/education/teachers/curricular-resources/elementary-school-curricular-resources/ask-not-what-your-country-can-do-for-you.

5. Audrey Hepburn, https://globalgreen.squarespace.com/blog/4616.

6. Jim Carrey, Maharishi University of Management Commencement speech, 2014; https://www.youtube.com/watch?v=V80-gPkpH6M.

24 | BREATH

1. Max Stromm, https://www.youtube.com/watch?v=4Lb5L-VEm34.

2. Timber Hawkeye, https://quotecatalog.com/quote/timber-hawkeye-you-cant-cal-Ra3mqb7.

3. Dr. Andrew Weil, https://www.youtube.com/watch?v=C20uniRyE4U.

25 | REVERENCE

1. Pema Chödrön,The Noble Journey From Fear to Fearlessness; https://www.youtube.com/watch?v=6t_SGso_1PY

2. Burgs, https://www.youtube.com/watch?v=_zpyg1QJp8Q.

3. Joseph Campbell, Ep. 4: Joseph Campbell and the Power of Myth— 'Sacrifice and Bliss' with BillMoyers.com; https://billmoyers.com/content/ep-4-joseph-campbell-and-the-power-of-myth-sacrifice-and-bliss-audio/.

4. Bob Newhart, https://www.goodreads.com/quotes/44284-All-i-can-say-about-life-is-oh-god-enjoy.

"When someone points at the moon,
Don't look at the finger."

~ Proverb

ABOUT THE AUTHOR

Linda Souders had one of those traditional American starts to life—born to a homemaker mother and an engineer father, raised by both, and a sales executive stepfather in the middle-class suburbs of Ohio where she went to school, marched to orders, tried to not make waves, and graduated with a B.F.A. from Miami University in Oxford, Ohio. For three decades she strived to create The Fairytale Picture by working as a graphic design art and creative director in Cincinnati, New York City and San Francisco, finding her Prince Charming, marrying, buying a home, having a beautiful baby, volunteering in her community, and doing all the things she was *supposed* to do. All the while she read voraciously the wisdom teachings of Joseph Campbell, Thích Nhất Hạnh, Pema Chödrön, Ram Dass, and many others. As her mental programs evolved, The Fairytale Picture disintegrated into divorce, and she was dragged by the fates into The Flow to become a certified holistic health educator and massage therapist (CMT), a registered yoga teacher (200-RYT), a master Journey meditation teacher, a national board-certified health and wellness coach (NB-HWC), and a writer. She passionately appreciates each moment of this never-ending personal evolution—this wild, exhilarating ride, called Life—mysteriously unfolding moment by moment. All the while, continually learning, growing, evolving, and passing on "the wisdom teachings" to help others far and wide.

ACKNOWLEDGMENTS

First, I acknowledge and thank the one Source
from which this book sprang.

Additionally, I thank the many faces of Source who showed up and were of service in helping this book be birthed into the world: all the many, many teachers throughout my life, too many to list, yet many are in this book, including Joseph Campbell, Pema Chödrön, Thích Nhất Hạnh, and Ram Dass who inspired me and helped me to navigate the ups and downs of my own authentic Path, thereby teaching me how to do it, and making it possible for me to pass the teachings on to others.

A big bow of thanks Tara Dale and Stephen Sokolar who saw the light in me when others couldn't, and invited me to teach; my fellow coach Dani Bois for helping to jump start the writing at a critical juncture; my friend and "rockstar" editor Todd Armstrong who shared his vast expertise and wisdom; to all the students who showed up to classes over the years and inspired me to gather and articulate much of the teachings that would later become this book; and to my daughter Alia for bringing so much life force and joy to the party.

A deep bow to Source, and all the faces of Source.

"It's all 'God.'"

Namaste.